EYEWITNESS
ROCKS & MINERALS

Opal

Slice from septarian nodule

Garnet-chlorite schist

Gypsum desert rose

Cinnabar

Hematite

Granite

Wenlock limestone with trilobite fossils

Cut tourmalines

EYEWITNESS
ROCKS & MINERALS

WRITTEN BY
Dr. R. F. SYMES
and the staff of the
Natural History Museum,
London

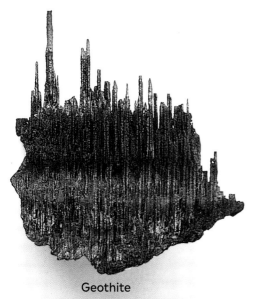
Geothite

Pyrite

Obsidian

Sulfur

Nephrite
"tiki"

Labradorite

In association with
THE NATURAL HISTORY MUSEUM

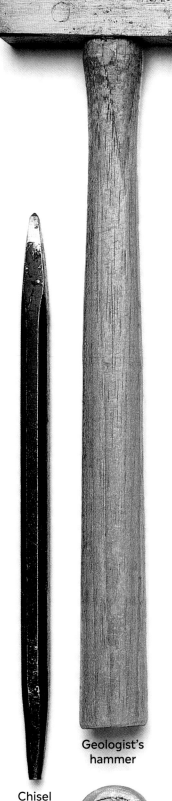

Geologist's
hammer

Chisel

Chalcedony cameo

REVISED EDITION
DK LONDON
Senior Editor Carron Brown
Senior Art Editor Lynne Moulding
US Editor Heather Wilcox
US Executive Editor Lori Cates Hand
Managing Editor Francesca Baines
Managing Art Editor Philip Letsu
Production Editor George Nimmo
Production Controller Samantha Cross
Jacket Design Development Manager Sophia MTT
Publisher Andrew Macintyre
Associate Publishing Director Liz Wheeler
Art Director Karen Self
Publishing Director Jonathan Metcalf

Consultant Cally Oldershaw

DK DELHI
Senior Editor Shatarupa Chaudhuri
Senior Art Editor Vikas Chauhan
Art Editors Sanya Jain, Sifat Fatima
Assistant Editor Sai Prasanna
Senior Picture Researcher Surya Sankash Sarangi
Managing Editor Kingshuk Ghoshal
Managing Art Editor Govind Mittal
Senior DTP Designer Neeraj Bhatia
DTP Designer Pawan Kumar
Jacket Designer Juhi Sheth

FIRST EDITION

Project Editor Janice Lacock
Art Editor Neville Graham
Managing Art Editor Jane Owen
Special Photography Colin Keates (Natural History
Museum, London) and Andreas Einsiedel
Editorial Consultants Dr. R. F. Symes
(Natural History Museum, London)
and Dr. Wendy Kirk (University College London)

This Eyewitness ® Guide has been conceived by
Dorling Kindersley Limited and Editions Gallimard

This American Edition, 2021
First American Edition, 1988
Published in the United States by DK Publishing
1450 Broadway, Suite 801, New York, NY 10018

A catalog record for this book is available from the Library of Congress.
ISBN 978-0-7440-3905-4 (Paperback)
ISBN 978-0-7440-2896-6 (ALB)

DK books are available at special discounts when purchased in bulk
for sales promotions, premiums, fund-raising, or educational use.
For details, contact: DK Publishing Special Markets,
1450 Broadway, Suite 801, New York, NY 10018
SpecialSales@dk.com

Printed and bound in China

For the curious
www.dk.com

MIX
Paper from
responsible sources
FSC™ C018179

This book was made with Forest Stewardship Council™ certified
paper—one small step in DK's commitment to a sustainable future.
For more information go to www.dk.com/our-green-pledge

Magnifying lens

Mixed rough
and polished
pebbles

Contents

Cut citrine

Clear topaz

Barite desert rose

Cut amethyst

WITHDRAWN

Our rocky planet

Earth is thought to be about 4,600 million years old. The word geology comes from the ancient Greek for Earth and study. The many different types of rocks found on our planet hold valuable details about Earth's long history, so geologists study them and figure out the processes and events that produced them.

Precious metals

Platinum, silver, and gold are valuable, rare metals.

Gold in quartz vein

Crystal habits

The shape of a crystal is known as its habit.

Cubes of pyrite

EARTH'S STRUCTURE

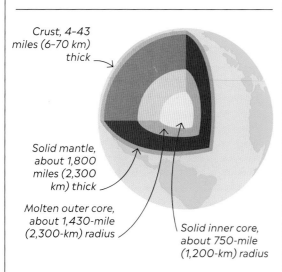

Crust, 4-43 miles (6-70 km) thick

Solid mantle, about 1,800 miles (2,300 km) thick

Molten outer core, about 1,430-mile (2,300-km) radius

Solid inner core, about 750-mile (1,200-km) radius

Earth consists of a core, mantle, and crust. The crust and upper mantle form vast plates that move slowly over the mantle beneath. The closer to the center of Earth, the greater the temperature and pressure.

Mineral ores

These are the sources of most useful metals.

Cassiterite (tin ore)

Cut citrine, a variety of quartz

Diamond in kimberlite

Gemstones

Rare, hard-wearing, and attractive minerals may be cut as gemstones, mainly for jewelry.

Quartz crystals

Crystals

Many minerals form regular-shaped solids with flat surfaces, known as crystals.

Fossils

These rocks contain the remains of, or impressions made by, former plants or animals.

MOVING PLATES

Where plates collide, mountain ranges may form. Where they pull apart, magma wells up to form deepsea ridges. Where one sinks beneath another, volcanoes erupt.

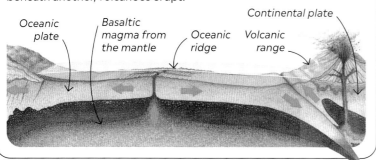

Oceanic plate

Basaltic magma from the mantle

Oceanic ridge

Continental plate

Volcanic range

Seashore pebbles
These are formed by the weathering of larger rocks by wave action.

Quartzite beach pebbles

Igneous rocks
The most common types of rocks have formed from molten magma.

Granite

Ganges River

Rocks and sediment flowing into sea

Bay of Bengal

Ganges Delta
India's Ganges River carries debris eroded from rocks and deposits it in the delta and sea. The debris may slowly form sedimentary rocks.

Volcanic rocks
Volcanic activity produces a number of different types of rocks and lava.

Hawaiian ropy lava

Lake Amboseli, a dry lake

Ingito Hills on edge of East African Rift Valley

Chyulu mountain range, Kenya

Carboniferous limestone

Sedimentary rocks
Rocks such as limestone, formed by the accumulation and compaction of loose sediments that have built up in layers, are called sedimentary rocks.

Anthracite, the hardest form of coal

Coal
One type of sedimentary rock, coal has formed from the fossilized remains of prehistoric plants.

Shelly limestone

Mount Meru *Mount Kilimanjaro* *Pangani River valley* *Glaciers of Kibo*

Landsat image of East Africa
This area shows a range of landscapes formed from different rocks, such as volcanic rocks forming volcanic Mount Kilimanjaro and evaporites in dried-up lakes.

Rocks and their minerals

Rocks are natural aggregates or combinations of one or more minerals. Some rocks contain only one mineral, but most consist of more. Minerals are inorganic solids with definite chemical compositions and an ordered atomic arrangement. Here, two common rocks—granite and basalt—are shown with specimens of the major minerals from which they are formed.

Granite and its major minerals

Minerals' size and texture vary with how a rock forms. In the coarse-grained rock granite, the major minerals are visible to the naked eye: quartz, mica, and feldspar.

Quartz

Mica

Feldspar

Quartz
These quartz crystals have milky, etched faces.

Etched face

Mica
Black biotite (a form of mica) crystals can be split into thin sheets.

Feldspar
Crystals of orthoclase (a feldspar) are pale pink or milky white.

Pyroxene
This well-developed, single black crystal of augite (a pyroxene) comes from Italy. Augite crystals are found in various igneous rocks.

Augite crystal

Rock matrix

Dark pyroxene

Basalt and its major minerals

The main minerals in basalt are olivine and pyroxene. The crystals in fine-grained basalt can sometimes be seen without a microscope. This olivine basalt was collected from volcanic rocks in Hawaii.

Olivine
Transparent crystals of olivine that are large enough to be used in jewelry are called "peridot."

Green olivine crystal

Diverse forms

Rocks are not always hard and resistant—loose sand and wet clay are considered to be rocks. The size of minerals in a rock ranges from millimeters in a fine-grained volcanic rock that cooled quickly to several meters in a rock such as a granite pegmatite that cooled slowly underground.

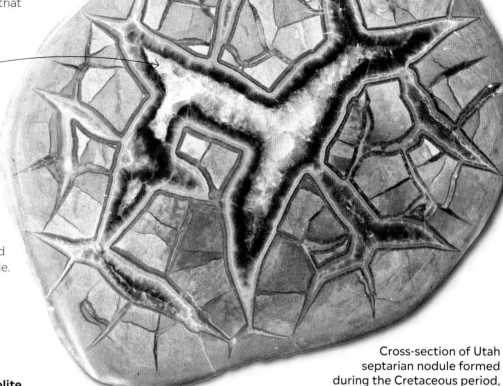

Yellow and white calcite crystallized in cracks

Rocks formed within rocks

This sedimentary rock specimen is a claystone septarian nodule. Nodules such as this form when groundwater redistributes minerals within a rock and forms a rounded nodule. This nodule has been taken out of the rock that surrounded it and broken open to show the yellow and white mineral calcite inside.

Cross-section of Utah septarian nodule formed during the Cretaceous period, 50–70 million years ago

Mesolite

Natural zeolites like this fine spray of mesolite crystals on rock form where volcanic rocks and ash layers react with groundwater.

 EYEWITNESS

Giant crystals

Giant gypsum crystals, some taller than a man, were discovered in 1999 in the Pulpí Geode, Spain, by Juan Garcia-Guinea. They formed from salty water underground. Evaporation of sea water leaves deposits of salt that can form evaporite rocks.

Lighter bands of pyroxene and plagioclase feldspar

Dark layer of chromite

Rocks that form in layers

Norite is an igneous rock made of the minerals pyroxene, plagioclase feldspar, and chromite. In this specimen, the dark and light minerals have separated into layers. The dark chromite layers constitute an important source of chromium.

Rock formation

Geological processes work in continual cycles, redistributing chemical elements, minerals, and rocks. These processes are driven by Earth's internal heat and, at its surface, by the sun's energy.

Andesite formed from a volcanic eruption in the Solomon Islands

Rocks from magma

Rocks formed within Earth from molten magma are called intrusive igneous rocks. Those that cooled slowly, deep under the surface (such as granite), are called plutonic, after Pluto, the Greek god of the underworld.

Granite

Gabbro, a basalt, from Finland

Volcanic activity

When rocks of the crust and upper mantle melt, they form magma, which volcanic activity brings to Earth's surface as extrusive igneous rocks. Basalt is the most common.

Ropy basaltic lava from Hawaii

Melting

Occasionally, high temperatures and pressures cause rocks to partially melt. If the rock is then squeezed, snaking veins may form. Migmatites are mixed rocks with a metamorphic host, such as gneiss or schist, cut by veins of granite.

Granite

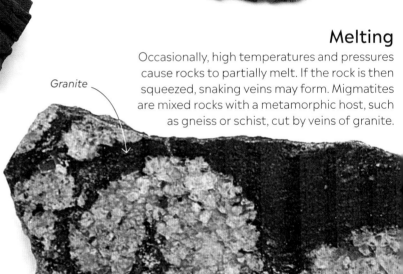

Igneous mountain

Sugar Loaf Mountain situated in Rio de Janeiro, Brazil, is made of intrusive igneous rocks. The softer rock that covered it has worn away to leave the mountain we see today.

Survivor

Le Puy de Dôme, France, is the plug once at the core of an ancient volcano.

Weathering

As wind, rain, ice, and heat act on rocks, they may lead to chemical changes or cause the rocks to fragment and form sediments, such as sand grains, clays, muds, and silt.

Pure quartz sand formed from weathered granites or sandstones

Clays produced by weathering are critical for soil formation

THE ROCK CYCLE

There is no starting point in this cycle, which has been going on for millions of years.

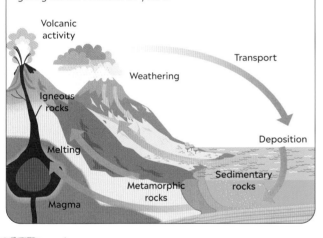

Sedimentary rocks

Sedimentary rocks are formed by the accumulation and compaction of loose sediments or other rocks that have been worn down. Sediments are transported by rivers, or by the wind in desert regions, and eventually deposited. They may build up in layers and may contain fossils.

Layered sandstone from the USA

Sedimentary banded claystone from Uganda

River transport

Rivers move rock debris from one area to another. Each day, the Mississippi River (right) deposits thousands of tons of debris into its delta.

Desert sandstone from Scotland

Metamorphic rocks

Quartz vein stands out in this schist rock face located in the Geoscope geological park in central France.

Gneiss

Mica schist formed from metamorphosed claystones

Gneiss, a banded metamorphic rock

Quartzite, a sandstone, altered by heat and pressure

Metamorphism

Rocks deep within Earth experience greater pressure from the overlying rocks and higher temperatures. Pressure and heat cause the rocks to change or "metamorphose" as the minerals recrystallize. The new rocks (such as gneiss, mica, and quartzite) are called metamorphic rocks.

Weathering and erosion

All rocks at Earth's surface break down. Weathering, chemical or mechanical, breaks them down where they are. Erosion breaks them down further as they are moved by the action of water, ice, or wind.

Wind erosion

Sediment-laden wind may slowly grind away at a rock.

Monument Valley, Utah and Arizona
Landscapes are changed by weathering and erosion. Wind has helped weather away the surrounding rock, leaving large "buttes" that look like monuments.

Abrasion by the wind
Softer layers of rock are worn away, leaving the harder ones protruding.

Sand blasting
Faceted sand-blown desert pebbles are called "dreikanters."

Weathering due to temperature

The expansion and contraction of rock as the temperature changes causes it to break up. Water expanding in the rock as it freezes can cause frost-shattering.

Sandstone made of sand accumulated 200 million years ago in a desert

Desert erosion
In deserts, where sediment is carried by wind, rocks are often reddish and composed of rounded sand grains.

Sand from a present-day desert in Saudi Arabia

Desert environment
Wind and temperature changes cause continual weathering, eventually breaking down rocks to barren sandy landscapes, such as here in the Sahara Desert.

Onion-skin weathering
Changes in temperature cause the surface layers of rock to expand, contract, and peel away.

Fine-grained rock

Peeling layers, like onion skins, expose the underlying rock

Onion-skin weathered rock

Chemical weathering

Minerals dissolved by acidic rainwater at the surface may be carried down into the soil and rock below.

Fresh, unaltered granite (left)

Granite tors, UK
Tors are weathered, rounded rocks left when surrounding rock has been eroded away.

Rock altered by percolating groundwater

Altered minerals
Granite is hard but becomes soft and crumbles after weathering.

Coarse, weathered granite

Secondary minerals

Chemical changes
These bright-colored "secondary minerals" were formed from deposits of dissolved minerals from weathered rocks higher up.

Tropical weathering
In the tropics, quartz is dissolved and carried off, while feldspars are changed to clay minerals that may form a surface deposit of bauxite.

Swiss glacier
Glaciers are a major cause of erosion in mountainous regions.

Ice erosion

As a glacier moves, it picks up fragments of rock, which form part of its icy base. The moving, frozen mass causes further erosion of underlying rocks.

Large rock fragment

Scratches caused by a glacier

Scratched rock
This limestone rock from Grindelwald, Switzerland, was scratched by fragments of harder rock in the glacier that flowed over it.

Glacier deposits
A till is a deposit left by a melting glacier and contains crushed rock fragments. Ancient tills formed into hard rock are called "tillite." This specimen is from the Flinders Ranges in South Australia, which was glaciated some 600 million years ago.

13

Rocks on the seashore

Many seashores are backed by cliffs. Coarse material that has fallen from above is gradually broken up by the sea and sorted into pebbles, gravel, sand, and mud. These various sizes are then deposited separately—to be recycled as different sedimentary rocks.

Large, coarse pebbles

Graded grains

On the beach, these pebbles are sorted by waves and tides. The sand is pure quartz—other minerals were washed away.

Skimming stones

The best skimming stones are disc-shaped and are probably sedimentary or metamorphic rocks, as they split into sheets.

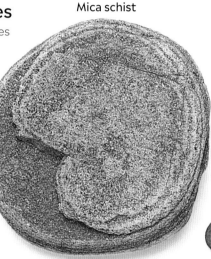

Mica schist

Slates

Irregularly shaped pyrite nodule

Hidden crystals

Pyrite nodules are common in chalk areas. The dull, knobby outside breaks open to reveal glistening crystals inside.

Local stones

These pebbles are metamorphic rocks that have been worn into flat discs on the beach where they were collected.

Amber pebbles

Amber is the fossil resin of extinct coniferous trees that lived thousands of years ago. It is especially common along the Baltic coasts of Russia and Poland.

Foreign material

Not all beach rocks are of local derivation. This porphyritic igneous rock was probably carried across the North Sea from Norway to England by ice during the last Ice Age.

Preserved waves

Visible at low tide, ripple marks form under water from sand carried by currents. This Finnish specimen preserves long-ago ripple marks in sandstone.

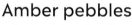

Black volcanic sands

In areas of volcanic activity, beach sand may be rich in dark minerals. The olivine sand comes from Scotland; the magnetite-bearing sand is from Tenerife.

Dark olivine sand

Magnetite-bearing sand

Black volcanic ash beach on north coast of Santorini, Greece

Medium-sized, coarse pebbles

Small, fine pebbles

Finest pebbles

Quartz sand

Marcasite interior reveals crystals radiating outward

Marcasite nodule, split in two

Found in chalk

Because flint nodules are hard, they resist abrasion and may be seen on beaches in chalk areas (right).

White Cliffs of Dover, UK

Granitic origin

In granite country, beach pebbles tend to be made of quartz, an abundant vein mineral, or pink or gray granite.

Flint nodules from below chalk cliffs

Assorted glass pebbles

Other pebbles

Over many years, trash such as glass and broken bricks can be worn and rounded by wave action.

Brick pebble

Igneous rock

These rocks form when magma from deep within Earth's crust and upper mantle cools and solidifies. Intrusive igneous rock solidifies underground and is later exposed by erosion. Magma that reaches Earth's surface and erupts is called extrusive igneous rock or volcanic rock.

Biotite granite

Black grains are biotite, a form of mica

Graphic granite

Long, angular quartz crystals look like ancient writing against the larger, pale-pink feldspar crystals

Red granite

Red coloring due to the high proportion of potassium feldspar in the rock

Granite

An extremely common intrusive rock, granite consists mainly of coarse grains of quartz, feldspar, and mica. The grains are large because they formed as the molten magma cooled slowly deep in Earth. Generally mottled, granite varies from gray to red, according to the different proportions of constituent minerals.

Pitchstone

Formed when volcanic lava cools very quickly, pitchstone contains some crystals of feldspar and quartz, but it has a dull, resinlike appearance and may be brown, black, or gray.

Obsidian

Like pitchstone, obsidian is a glass formed from rapidly cooled lava. It forms so quickly, there is no time for crystals to grow. Its characteristically sharp edges made it useful as an early tool.

Giant's Causeway

When basaltic lava cools, it often forms hexagonal columns. Around 40,000 such basaltic columns form the Giant's Causeway in Northern Ireland. These interlocking pillars were formed nearly 60 million years ago.

Phenocryst
of feldspar

Feldspar porphyry

Porphyries are rocks that contain large crystals called "phenocrysts" within a medium-grained rock. This particular sample contains feldspar crystals and comes from Wales.

Gabbro

An intrusive rock, gabbro consists of dark minerals, such as olivine and augite. It has coarse grains, as large crystals formed when the magma slowly cooled.

Calcite vein

Serpentinite

This coarse-grained, red and green rock is named after its dominant mineral, serpentine. It is streaked with white veins of calcite. Serpentinite is common in the Alps.

Basalt

Formed from solidified lava, basalt is the most common extrusive rock. It is similar in composition to gabbro but finer grained. When the lava cools, it may split into many-sided columns, as seen at St. Helena's Needle and Northern Ireland's Giant's Causeway.

Vesicular volcanic rocks

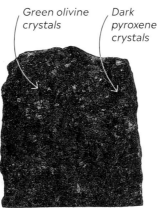

In the volcanically active islands of Hawaii, vesicular volcanic rocks formed when bubbles of gas were trapped in hot lava scum. Vesicular basalt is light and full of holes known as "vesicles." In amygdaliodal basalt (shown here), the holes were later filled in with minerals.

Green olivine crystals

Dark pyroxene crystals

Peridotite

A dark, heavy rock mainly containing the minerals olivine and pyroxene, peridotite is thought to lie under layers of gabbro 6 miles (10 km) beneath the ocean floor.

👁 EYEWITNESS

Quartz crystal cluster
The world's largest known quartz crystal cluster was discovered in 1985 in the Otjua mine in Namibia. The excavation took three years. It weighs 15.5 tons (14,100 kg) and is 10 ft (3 m) high, almost twice the height of a person. It is on display at the Kristall Galerie in Namibia.

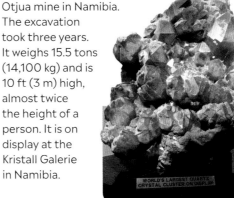

Volcanic rock

Rocks formed by volcanic activity can be divided into pyroclastic rocks and lavas. The first are formed from either solid rock fragments or "bombs" of lava that solidify as they fly through the air. Lavas may be thick, sticky, and flow very slowly. More fluid, fast-flowing lavas spread out over vast areas.

Ejection of lava from Eldfell, Iceland, 1973

Pyroclastic rocks

Pyroclastic rocks consist of rock and lava pieces that were blown apart by exploding gases.

Volcanic bombs are shaped while they fly through the air

Agglomerate formed close to a vent

Volcanic bombs
When blobs of lava are thrown out of a volcano, some solidify in the air and land on the ground as hard "bombs." These two specimens are shaped like footballs, because they spun in the air, but bombs may be spherical or irregular in appearance.

Intrusion breccia formed within a vent

Jumbled pieces
The force of an explosion may cause rocks to fragment. The angular pieces land inside or close to the vent and form rocks known as agglomerates.

INSIDE A VOLCANO

Magma flows through a central vent or side vents. Underground, it may form dykes that cut across rock layers or sills parallel to them.

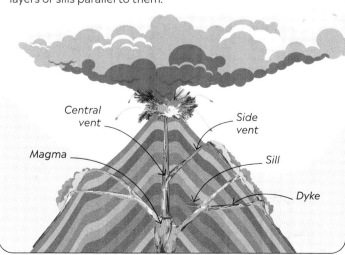

Central vent

Magma

Side vent

Sill

Dyke

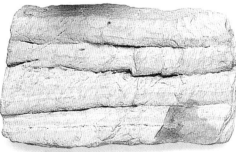

Bedded tuff (a hardened ash)

Ash

Wind-blown particles
Volcanic ash can travel thousands of miles in the atmosphere. Where it settles and hardens, it forms tuff. When Mount St. Helens erupted in 1980, coarse grains were blown 3 miles (5 km); fine particles were wind-carried 17 miles (27 km).

Eruption of Mount St. Helens, Washington State, 1980

Vesuvius, 79 CE

This famous eruption produced a *nuée ardente*, a fast-moving cloud of magma and ash, and destroyed the Roman town of Pompeii.

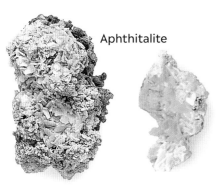

Aphthitalite

Rocks from gases

Inactive volcanoes are called "dormant," but escaping volcanic gases may form minerals, such as yellow sulfur and blue aphthitalite.

Viscous lavas

These sticky lavas may erupt or solidify in the volcano's vent, trap gases, and erupt explosively, producing pyroclastic rocks, volcanic bombs, and ash.

Floating rocks

Pumice is solidified lava froth. Because the froth contains bubbles of gas, the rock is peppered with holes. Pumice is the only rock that floats in water.

Grains of rhyolite are very small

Molasses-like lavas

This light-colored pink or gray, extrusive igneous rock is called rhyolite. The distinctive bands formed as the sticky, viscous lava flowed for short distances.

Natural glass

Although chemically the same as pumice, obsidian has a different texture. Obsidian is a natural glass that cooled too quickly for crystals to form. Because of its sharp edges, primitive humans used it for tools, arrowheads, and ornaments.

Basaltic lavas

These lavas flow smoothly, forming flatter volcanoes or welling up through cracks in the ocean floor. As a result, the vent does not get choked, and gases can escape. Volcanoes with basaltic lavas are not as explosive as those with viscous lavas, and although there is plenty of lava, gases can escape, and few pyroclastic rocks are formed.

Runny lavas

Basaltic lavas are fast-flowing and so quickly spread out to cover vast areas. This specimen of basalt was deposited by the Hualalai volcano on Hawaii.

Colorful crystals

Sparkling points in this basalt include green olivine and black pyroxene crystals.

Ropy lava

As lava flows, the surface cools and forms a skin that wrinkles as the fluid center continues to flow.

Sedimentary rock

Weathered and eroded rocks break into smaller pieces of rock and minerals. This sediment may be transported to a new site (often a lake, river, or sea) and deposited in layers that become buried and compacted. Cemented together, the particles form new, sedimentary rocks.

Evaporites

Some sedimentary rocks are formed when saline waters (often seawater) evaporate and leave deposits of minerals. Examples include halite and gypsum. We get table salt from halite (rock salt). Gypsum, used in plaster of Paris, is called alabaster in its massive form.

Gypsum crystals growing from a central point like daisy petals

Gypsum

Clay

Formed of microscopically fine grains, clay feels sticky when wet. When it is compacted and all the water is forced out, it forms hard rocks called mudstone or shale.

Hole-filled, irregular-shaped rock

Halite

Reddish cast caused by impurities in the salt

Calcareous tufa

An extraordinary-looking evaporite, this porous rock is formed by the evaporation of spring water and is sometimes found in limestone caves.

Sandstones

Grains of sand cemented together form sandstones. The red sandstone comes from a desert, where wind rubbed and rounded the quartz grains. Grit is rougher—its more angular grains were buried before they could be rubbed smooth.

Grit

Red sandstone

Bedded volcanic ash

In many sedimentary rocks, individual layers of sediments form visible bands. Here, the stripes are layers of volcanic ash. The surface has been polished to highlight this feature.

Rock builders

Foraminifera are microscopic marine organisms that secrete lime. When they die, the shells fall to the ocean floor, where they eventually become chalk and may become cemented to form limestone.

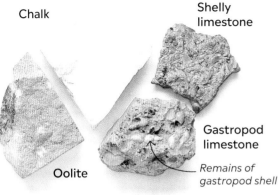

Chalk

Oolite

Shelly limestone

Gastropod limestone

Remains of gastropod shell

Flint
A form of silica (like quartz), lumps of flint are often found in limestone, especially chalk. They are gray or black but may be covered in a white, powderlike material. Like obsidian, when flint is broken, it has a "conchoidal" fracture.

Ammonite in limestone
Ammonite shells often show up against the mud that buried them. Ammonites are now extinct. This fossil was found in limestone.

Limestones

Many sedimentary rocks consist of the remains of organisms. In these shelly and gastropod limestones, the remains of animals are clearly visible in the rock. Chalk is also a limestone, formed from the skeletons of tiny sea animals too small to see with the naked eye. Oolite, another limestone, forms in the sea as calcite builds up around grains of sand. As they are rolled back and forth by waves, the grains become larger.

Algal limestone
"Muddy" limestones, like this one bound together by algae, are also called "landscape marbles"—when the minerals crystallize, they may produce patterns in the shapes of trees and bushes.

Sedimentary layers
The Grand Canyon, in Arizona, is a UNESCO World Heritage Site, carved out over millions of years by the Colorado River as it weathered and eroded the rocks. The sides of the canyon are mainly layers of softer sedimentary rocks, including limestone, sandstone, mudstone, and shale, above a harder, older basement of mainly metamorphic rock.

Flint pebble

Conglomerate
The flint pebbles in this rock were rounded by water as they were rolled about on river or sea beds. After they were buried, they became cemented together to form a rock known as conglomerate.

Breccia
Like conglomerate, breccias contain fragments of rock; however, these are much more angular as they have not been rounded by water or carried far from their original home – often at the bottom of cliffs.

Limestone

Limestone caves, lined with dripping stalactites and giant stalagmites, are formed when slightly acidic rainwater changes the limestone's chemistry. This makes it possible for the rock to dissolve in water and be washed away.

Tufa

A type of rock known as a precipitate, tufa forms when lime is deposited from water onto a rock surface in areas of low rainfall.

Coral-like structure

Plan de Sales, France

Limestone pavements of flat blocks occur where weathering leaves no insoluble residue to make soil.

LIMESTONE LANDSCAPES

Rainwater dissolves calcite in limestone, producing deep, narrow cracks ("grikes"). In time, the water enlarges them into passages. Flowing water dissolves the rock, producing "swallow holes" at the junctions between grikes. Underground streams form lakes in the caves.

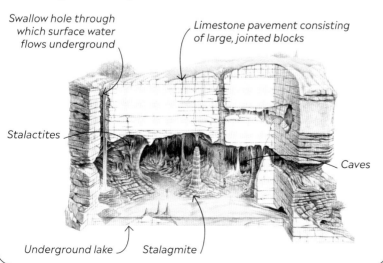

Swallow hole through which surface water flows underground

Limestone pavement consisting of large, jointed blocks

Stalactites

Caves

Underground lake

Stalagmite

Stone Forest, China

The staggering landscape of the Hunan Province of China is typical of "karst" scenery. Named after the limestone area of Karst in Yugoslavia, the term is applied to many limestone regions, including the Cumberland Plateau, Tennessee; parts of the Blue Mountains, Australia; and the Causses, France.

 Top section attached to the roof of the cave

Stalactites

Stalactites are formed in caves by groundwater containing dissolved lime dripping from the roof and leaving a deposit as it evaporates. Growing downward a tiny fraction of an inch each year—shown in annual growth rings—they may slowly reach many feet in length.

Stalactites may take hundreds of years to form

The newest growth is at the bottom

Pamukkale Falls, Turkey

Beautiful travertine terraces are formed from the precipitation of calcite from hot springs in limestone areas. Travertine is quarried as a decorative building stone.

Point onto which overhead drips fall

Stalagmites

Stalagmites are formed on the floor of caves where water has dripped from the roof or a stalactite above. As with stalactites, they develop as water containing dissolved lime evaporates. If stalactites and stalagmites grow together and join, forming pillars, they are often described as "organ pipes," "hanging curtains," and "portcullises."

Metamorphism

Metamorphic rocks are igneous or sedimentary rocks altered by heat and/or pressure. Such conditions can occur during the mountain-building process, as buried rocks are subjected to high temperatures and squeezed or folded, creating new minerals.

Saccharoidal marble

Nodular gray marble

Pyroxene-bearing marble

Marbles

When limestone is exposed to very high temperatures, new crystals of calcite grow and form the compact rock known as marble. This can look similar to the rock quartzite, but marble is softer and easily scratched with a knife. Some medium-grained marble looks sugary or "saccharoidal."

Eclogite

Produced under very high pressure, eclogite is extremely dense and is thought to form in the mantle—far deeper than most other rocks. It contains pyroxene and small, red crystals of garnet.

Spotted slate

Aggregates of carbon

Spotted hornfels

From slate to hornfels

The irregular speckles in spotted slate are small aggregates of carbon, formed by heat from an igneous intrusion. In rocks closer to the intrusion, the temperature is considerably higher, and needlelike crystals of chiastolite form in the slate. The rocks become so hot that they recrystallize and form a tough, new rock called hornfels.

Chiastolite slate

Elongated chiastolite crystals

Red garnet crystals

Slate

During mountain building, shale was squeezed so hard that its flaky micas crystallized at right angles to the pressure. The resultant rock—slate—splits easily into thin sheets.

White muscovite mica

Green chlorite mineral

Garnet-muscovite-chlorite schist

Schists

Schist is formed from shale or mud but at a higher temperature than slate. The garnet-muscovite-chlorite schist was exposed to temperatures of at least 932°F (500°C). Kyanite-staurolite schist forms under high pressure, 6–9 miles (10–15 km) below ground.

Blue, bladelike crystals of kyanite

Kyanite-staurolite schist

Pink granitic rock

Dark host rock

Crystals of a green variety of pyroxene

Migmatite

Under intense heat, parts of rocks may start to melt and flow, creating swirling patterns. This is very often shown in migmatites. They are composed of not one rock but a mixture of a dark host rock with lighter-colored granitic rock. This sample is from the Scottish Highlands.

Light-colored layer containing quartz and feldspar

Banded gneiss

Biotite-kyanite gneiss

Black biotite crystals

Dark band of biotite

Gneisses

At high temperatures and pressures, sedimentary or igneous rocks may be metamorphosed to gneisses. These rocks have coarser grains than medium-grained schists and bands of varying minerals. These layers may be irregular where the rock has been folded under pressure.

Blue kyanite crystals

Marble

Marble is a metamorphosed limestone, but its name is often used in the stone industry for a variety of other rocks. All are valued for their attractive range of textures and colors, and because they are easily cut and polished.

In the raw
A true marble, this unpolished, coarsely crystalline specimen of Mijas Marble is from Malaga, Spain. Polishing will give it a smooth surface.

The marble from Carrara was used to make iconic buildings, such as the Pantheon in Rome

Carrara quarry
The world's most famous marble comes from the Carrara quarry in Tuscany, Italy. It was the local stone for Michelangelo.

Italian speciality
Gray Bardilla marble (left) comes from the Carrara quarry.

Greek connection
Originally from the Greek Island of Euboea, streaked Cipollino marble (above) is now quarried in Switzerland, the island of Elba, and Vermont.

Italian elegance
Another striking Italian marble (right) is the black and gold variety from Liguria.

Tuscan stones

The distinctive texture of the Italian decorative stone Breccia Violetto was the reason for its use in the Paris Opera House in 1875.

Taj Mahal, India

Built by around 20,000 artisans, this monument is made of ivory-white marble.

Detail of marble inlay on the Taj Mahal

South African swirls

Polished travertine has beautiful swirling patterns. This piece is from Cape Province, South Africa.

Swiss origins

The limestone breccia known as Macchia-vecchia is quarried in Mendrisio, Switzerland.

African copper

Quarried in Swaziland, Green Verdite's vivid color is caused by the presence of copper.

Algerian rock

Breche Sanguine or Red African (bottom) is a red breccia from Algeria. The Romans used it in the Pantheon in the 1st century CE.

The first **flint tools**

Because flint splits in any direction, fractures to a sharp edge, and is fairly widespread, it was used in prehistoric times to make tools and weapons.

Leather thong securing flint and antler sleeve to handle

Crude early chopper

Rough cutting edge

TOOLS FROM FLINT

Flint tools were shaped by striking a flint nodule or fragment with another stone or hitting it against a rock to break off flakes of flint.

Stone-on-stone
Striking the flint with a stone created sharp, jagged edges.

Pressure-flaking
Pointed implements such as antler bones gave tools sharper cutting edges.

Sharp-pointed flint tool used for cutting the skin from animals

Sharp-edged flint tool used for scraping and preparing the animal skins for use

Hand axes

Palaeolithic hand axes were used to smash animal bones, skin hunted animals, and cut wood and plants. The well-developed, dark ax is 70,000–300,000 years old. The lighter-colored ax dates to around 70,000–35,000 BCE.

Large, sharpened hand ax

Light-colored hand ax

Cutting edge

Dark-colored hand ax

Early men using hand axes

Flint flakes and chippings

Sharp cutting edge

Sharp cutting edge

Mesolithic adz

Antler sleeve

Ninth-century obsidian ax from Mexico

Obsidian

Like flint, obsidian was used in early tools because it breaks with sharp edges.

Spearhead with obsidian blade from the Admiralty Islands, off Papua New Guinea

Cutting edge of flint

Adz from the Mesolithic period (10,000–4000 BCE)

Flint mounted directly onto handle

Reproduction wooden handle

Modern wooden handle

Danish ax and dagger

Ax

Flint dagger

The shape of this Early Bronze Age ax, found in the Thames River in the UK, shows it was imported. Polished with care, it was clearly an object of value. So, too, was the Early Bronze Age flint dagger (2300–1200 BCE).

Arrowheads

The bow and arrow was invented in the Mesolithic period and was still used for hunting in the Early Neolithic period, when leaf-shaped arrowheads were common. Later, in the Beaker period (2750–1800 BCE), barbed arrowheads were characteristic.

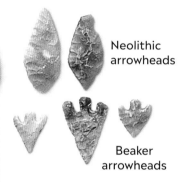

Neolithic arrowheads

Beaker arrowheads

Sickle

Flint sickles show crops were cultivated. The long, slightly curved blade was swung from side to side to harvest crops. A "gloss" on their cutting edge shows repeated harvesting. This one is Neolithic (4000–2300 BCE).

Woodworker shaping a chair leg using a modern adz

Adz is held by the handle and swung up and down

Cutting edge of an adz

Flint daggers

Rare and made with care, these two daggers from the Beaker period were not just weapons but status symbols too.

Hafted adzes

Adzes were made by fitting a shaped flint directly to a handle made of wood or antler. The cutting edge of an adz cuts or chops meat and wood. Adzes are still used in the modern day in agriculture and furniture making.

29

Rocks as tools

Archaeologists have found lots of rocks that have been shaped by people from many different cultures around the world. Some were used as weapons or status symbols, others as farming or household tools.

Brazilian stone ax

Neolithic ax showing a highly polished surface

Neolithic ax made of diorite, an igneous rock

Neolithic ax made of rhyolitic tuff, a volcanic rock

Stone axes

These stone axes date back to Neolithic Britain (4000–2300 BCE). Highly polished and tougher than flaked flint axes, they were traded over long distances—the source rocks were far from the places where the axes were found.

Wedge to stop the stone from moving

Bored quartzite pebble

Digging stick

During the Mesolithic and Neolithic periods (10,000–2300 BCE), sticks weighted with pierced pebbles were used to break up the ground to plant crops or dig up roots.

Reproduction wooden stick

Sharpened wooden point for digging hard ground

South African digging stick with horn point and stone weight

Breaking up ground with a digging stick prior to planting

Ax end

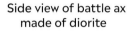

Side view of battle ax made of diorite

Top view of battle ax

Hammer end

Dual-purpose granite ax-hammer

Battle axes

These axes with holes in them are from the Early Bronze Age (2300–1200 BCE) and are so well preserved that they could have been status symbols for display as well as for use as weapons. The bottom one was both an ax and a hammer.

👁 **EYEWITNESS**

Stone maul

This carved stone maul (a war club or mace) in the form of a bird's head was made by Haida Indians. The Haida are a North American tribe who live on islands off British Columbia. They are known for their craftsmanship and trading skills.

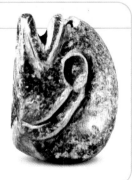

Whetstones

Bronze implements were sharpened by rubbing the blunt edge against a whetstone. These two are Bronze Age (2300–700 BCE) and were worn on a cord.

Engraved Viking forge stone made of soapstone and used in metalworking

A bird-shaped mortar carved by Haida Indians

Marble make-up palette

Romans used powdered lead and chalk to whiten skin, red ocher to tint lips and cheeks, and soot to darken eyebrows. Small amounts were put on a stone palette or in a stone bowl and mixed with water, tree resin (gum), or egg white to make a colored paint or paste.

Stone spindle whorl

Stone whorl with a hole

To spin wool or cotton into thread, the Romans weighted a bone or wooden spindle with a stone whorl. The weight and rotating motion help twist the thread, which was then wound on to the spindle.

Handle

Hole for the grain

Roman rotary quern

A quern was used for grinding corn between two stones. The upper one was held in place by a spindle and was rotated by a handle. Grain was fed through the hole in the upper stone, and the rotary motion forced it between the two grinding surfaces.

Upper stone is rotated using the handle

Grain is crushed between the stones

Grain ready for grinding

Lower stone does not move

Pigments

For body and rock art, early humans crushed local rocks and mixed the powders with animal fats to produce a range of pigments. Over the centuries, as trading routes grew, artists had new colors to work with.

Brown clay

Powdered brown clay

Earthy hues
Clays were widely used by early artists because they were easy to find, soft, and easy to crush.

Green clay

Powdered green clay

Umber paint

Ocher paint

Color variation in a mineral
Many minerals are uniformly colored, but some come in a range of colors. For example, tourmaline (above) may occur as black, brown, pink, green, and blue crystals or show a variety of colors in a single crystal.

White chalk

Shades of white
The first white pigment was chalk or, in some areas, kaolin (china clay) instead.

Powdered chalk

Cave painting image

Cave painting
The earliest known artworks were made with a mixture of clays, chalk, dirt, and burned wood and bones.

Black charcoal from the embers of fire

Orange and brown ocher

Chalk white paint

Bison from Grotte de Niaux, France, c. 20,000 BCE

Color clues
A useful aid when identifying a mineral is the color that it produces when you crush it. Or simply scrape a sample across an unglazed white tile—many minerals leave a distinct, colored streak, which may or may not be the same color as the mineral; others have no discernible streak.

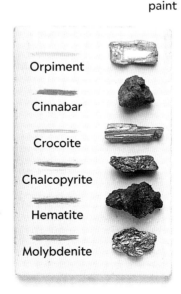

Orpiment

Cinnabar

Crocoite

Chalcopyrite

Hematite

Molybdenite

Black as coal
Still popular with artists today, charcoal was well known to cave painters—from the embers of their fires.

Powdered charcoal

Lampblack paint

Iron red

The earthy variety of hematite, an iron ore, produces a rich reddish-brown pigment. Very finely powdered, it was also used as makeup for skin.

Powdered hematite

Red paint

Powdered realgar

Egyptian orange

About 1,500 BCE, Egyptians first crushed realgar, an arsenic compound found in hot spring deposits, to form an orange pigment.

Arsenic orange paint

Powdered orpiment

Powdered malachite

Brilliant green

Bronze-Age Egypt first used malachite, a copper compound, for green.

Malachite Green paint

Bright gold

Medieval artists used orpiment, an arsenic compound, to make many colors and to imitate gold.

King's yellow paint

Ultramarine paint

Powdered lapis lazuli

Precious blue

The rich blue (and expensive) ultramarine paint was called "Persian blue," as it was originally made in Iran (formerly called Persia) from Persian lapis lazuli.

Powdered azurite

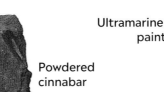

Powdered cinnabar

Classical blue

The copper compound azurite produced a highly prized blue pigment that was widely used in classical antiquity.

Azurite blue paint

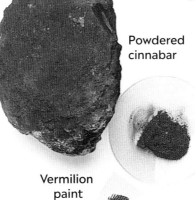

Intense red

The bright, vermilion red of cinnabar (mercuric sulfide) was used in prehistoric China but only came into widespread use in the Middle Ages.

Vermilion paint

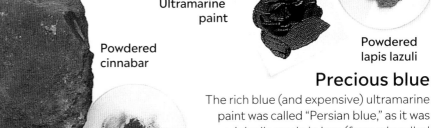

Modern ocher

More than 70,000 years ago, our Stone Age ancestors used natural rock pigments such as ocher to make cave paintings. In the 19th century, Dutch artist Van Gogh used ocher in his still-life paintings.

Building stones

Most of the great monuments of the past survive because they were made from tough, natural stone. Generally, local stone was used, but sometimes stone was transported long distances and even across seas for building projects.

Quarrying in the early 19th century was still done almost entirely by manual labor.

Nummulitic limestone

Formed 40 million years ago, nummulite is a famous limestone made up of fossils called foraminifera.

The pyramids at Giza, Egypt, were made of local nummulite limestone.

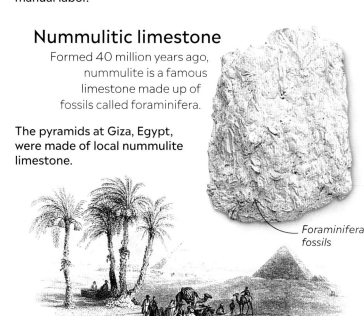

Foraminifera fossils

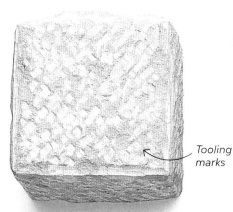

Tooling marks

Portland stone

After the Great Fire of London in 1666, St. Paul's Cathedral was rebuilt with this English limestone. The marks are made by "tooling," a decorative technique.

Granite

Polished granite is often used to cover large buildings, as in much of the imperial city of St. Petersburg, Russia.

Christian mosaic

Small fragments of local stones were often used for mosaic floors.

160-million-year-old limestone used for roofing

Welsh slate

Slate

Unlike most building materials, roofing stones must split easily into thin sheets. Slate is ideal, but where it was not available, builders used local, often inferior, stone.

Notre Dame, Paris
This famous cathedral in Paris, France, was built from local limestone from the St. Jacques region of the city, between 1163 and 1250. The catacombs in Paris are old quarries.

Sandstones
Various colored sandstones make excellent building stones, as seen in many fine Mogul monuments in India.

Oolitic limestone
This building stone formed some 160 million years ago.

230-million-year-old sandstone

Red sandstone from Scotland used to give a covering layer to buildings

Pantile

Interlocking roof tile

Materials
Many modern buildings are made of bricks, tiles, cement, concrete, and glass (from silica sand).

Roofing tiles
In many parts of the world, roofing tiles are made from clay.

Textured buff brick

Skyscrapers
New York skyscrapers are made of granite, sandstone, and manufactured materials.

Bricks
Easily molded clays are fired to make bricks. Impurities in clays produce various colors and strengths.

Smooth red brick

Cement
It is made by grinding and heating limestone. Cement mixed with sand, gravel, and water produces concrete.

Great Wall of China
The world's biggest construction, 1,500 miles (2,400 km) long, uses various natural and manufactured materials that change with the landscape it passes through. Parts include brick, granite, and various local rocks.

The story of coal

The coal we burn is millions of years old. In the swampy forests of Asia, Europe, and North America, rotting leaves, seeds, and dead wood became buried. Overlying sediments squeezed the water out and compressed the plant matter into peat and then coal, layer upon layer. As pressure and heat grew, other types of coals were formed.

Plant roots

Fossilized wood
Jet is hard, black, but very light and is derived from driftwood laid down in the sea. Polished and carved, often for jewelry, it has been used since the Bronze Age.

Coal as jewelry
A major source of jet is Yorkshire, in northern England. These Roman pendants, found in York, were probably made of local jet.

Oil shale
A sedimentary rock, oil shale contains kerogen, an organic substance of plant and animal origin. The rock smells of oil, and when heated, kerogen gives off a vapor from which oil is extracted.

Leaf

Stalk

Seed case

The beginning of the story

In areas with thick layers of vegetation and poor drainage, such as swamps or bogs, dead plants become waterlogged. They start to rot but cannot decay completely.

The origins of coal

Carboniferous swamps may have looked similar to this black-and-white drawing.

The peat layer

Peat is a more compact form of the surface layer of rotting plants. Some roots and seed cases are still visible. Newly formed peat can be cut, dried, and burned as a fuel.

Cutting peat

This Irish turf-cutter is using traditional methods, but others use big machines.

Brown coal

Naturally compressed peat forms crumbly, brown lignite that still contains recognizable plant remains. Undried peat is 90 percent water; lignite is 50 percent.

Deposit of coal within layers of rock

Coal seams

Layers of coal are called seams. They are sandwiched between layers of other material, such as sandstones and mudstones.

"Black gold"

Under pressure, lignite is converted into bituminous or household coal. Hard and brittle, it has a very high carbon content. A charcoal-like powdery substance makes the coal dirty to handle.

Children in a mine, 1842

During the Industrial Revolution, miners and their children worked long hours underground, in terrible conditions.

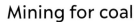

Mining for coal

Coal has been mined since the Middle Ages. Some mines are open-cast, at the surface, but most are several hundred yards beneath the land or sea.

The hardest coal

The highest-quality coal is anthracite. Shiny, harder than other coals, and clean to touch, it contains more carbon than the others, and it gives out the most heat and little smoke.

Fossils

Fossils are the evidence of past life preserved in the rocks of Earth's crust. When an animal or plant is buried in sediment, usually the soft parts rot away, but the hardest parts remain—most fossils consist of the bones or shells of animals or the leaves or woody parts of plants. In some marine fossils, shells may be replaced by other minerals, or an impression of the insides or outsides may be preserved. Fossils are found in sedimentary rocks, especially limestones and shales.

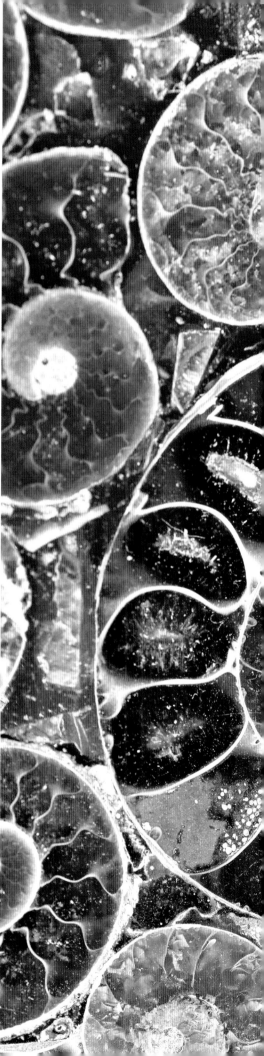

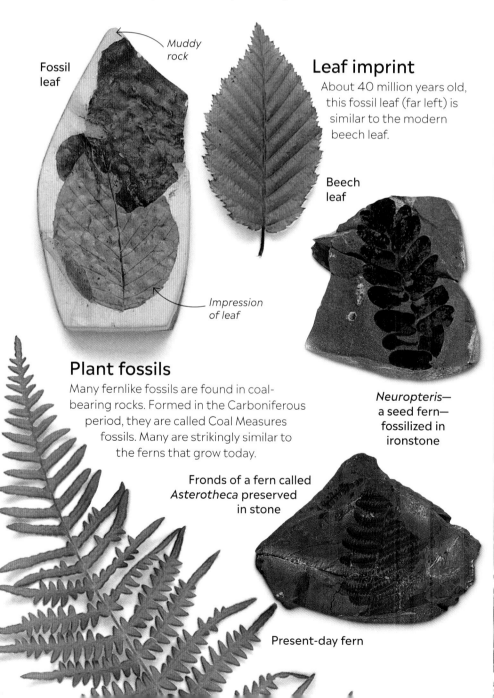

Muddy rock

Fossil leaf

Leaf imprint
About 40 million years old, this fossil leaf (far left) is similar to the modern beech leaf.

Beech leaf

Impression of leaf

Plant fossils
Many fernlike fossils are found in coal-bearing rocks. Formed in the Carboniferous period, they are called Coal Measures fossils. Many are strikingly similar to the ferns that grow today.

Neuropteris—a seed fern—fossilized in ironstone

Fronds of a fern called *Asterotheca* preserved in stone

Present-day fern

Ancient ancestors

Ammonites were sea creatures that had hard, coiled shells and are now extinct. Because ammonites changed rapidly and lived in many areas of the world, they can be used to determine the relative ages of the rocks in which they occur. The nearest modern equivalent to the ammonite is the nautilus.

Buried bones

Dinosaur bones buried in sediments such as mud may slowly turn into rock. The fossil bones may be replaced by minerals, such as calcite and silica.

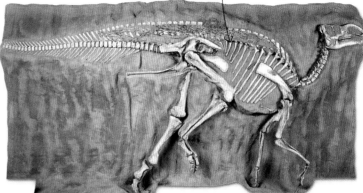

Skeleton partially embedded in rock

Fossilized skeleton of *Gryposaurus*

Fossil hunting

The abundance of fossils on seashores made collecting a popular pastime in the 19th century.

Garden snails

A graveyard for snails

This piece of limestone contains the hard spiral shells of marine gastropods (snails) from about 120 million years ago.

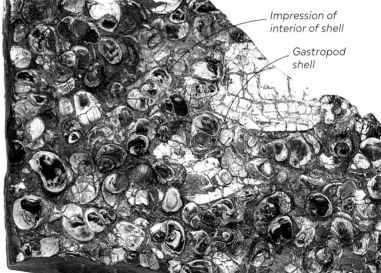

Impression of interior of shell

Gastropod shell

Space rocks

Thousands of meteorites that weigh more than 1 lb (450 g) fall to Earth every year; most land in the sea or on deserts. Only a few are recovered annually. As they enter Earth's atmosphere, their surfaces may melt and form a crust, protecting the stony or metallic interior.

Gray interior consisting mainly of the minerals olivine and pyroxene

Fragment of a stony meteorite

Pasamonte fireball

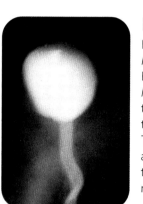

Photographed in New Mexico, this fireball fell to Earth in March 1933. Meteorites are named after the places where they fall—this one in Pasamonte. The fireball broke up in the atmosphere, leading to the fall of dozens of meteoritic stones.

Dark, glassy fusion crust formed during passage through Earth's atmosphere

Earth's contemporary

The meteorite above fell at Barwell, Leicestershire, UK, on Christmas Eve, 1965. It formed 4,600 million years ago, at the same time as Earth but in another part of the solar system. Of every ten meteorites seen to fall, eight are "stones" like Barwell.

Iron meteorite

The Canon Diablo meteorite is an iron meteorite that fell to Earth about 20,000 years ago in Arizona. Iron meteorites are made of iron and nickel from the core of the asteroid. The Earth's core is also made of iron and nickel.

Metal and stone

Stony-irons form a separate group of meteorites. This slice of the Thiel Mountains meteorite (below) shows bright metal enclosing stony material. It was found in Antarctica, where meteorites have lain for about 300,000 years, largely encased in ice.

Explosion crater

The Canon Diablo meteorite weighed 16,535 tons (15,000 metric tons). On landing, it exploded leaving about 33 tons (30 metric tons) of meteorite fragments scattered in the area. The explosion left a large circular hole about 0.75 mile (1.2 km) across and nearly 600 ft (180 m) deep, named Meteor Crater.

Nickel-iron metal part

Stony part

Crystals of the mineral olivine

Nickel-iron metal

Stony part

Fragment of a pallasite type stony-iron meteorite

Halley's Comet

Water-bearing meteorites may have come from comets, such as Halley's—here depicted in the 11th-century Bayeux tapestry.

Fragments of stardust that predate our solar system have been found in this rock

ASTEROID STRUCTURE

Many meteorites come from the collision of asteroids that orbit the sun. The type of meteorite that lands on Earth depends on which part of the asteroid reaches us: iron meteorites, like Canon Diablo, are from the core of the asteroid; stony-iron meteorites, like Thiel Mountains, are from the core-mantle; and stony meteorites, like Barwell, are from the crust.

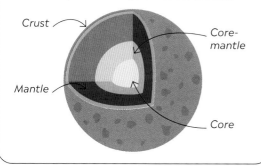

Crust

Core-mantle

Mantle

Core

Water bearers

The Murchison meteorite fell in Australia in 1969. It contains carbon compounds and water, similar to the nucleus of a comet. Such meteorites are rare.

Meteorite contains dozens of amino acids, many of which are not found on Earth

Rocks from the moon and Mars

Five meteorites found in Antarctica are known to have come from the moon because they are like lunar highlands rocks collected by the Apollo missions. Eight other meteorites are thought to have come from Mars.

Mars meteorite

The Nakhla stone fell in Egypt in 1911. Only 1,300 million years old, far younger than most meteorites, it probably came from Mars.

Moon rocks

Almost 400 moon rocks (lunar meteorites) have been discovered on Earth. They are fragments of more than 30 different meteorite falls. Scientists know they come from the moon because they compared these meteorites with moon rocks that were brought back from the lunar highlands to Earth by astronauts such as Jack Schmitt on the Apollo 17 mission.

Jack Schmitt on the moon

Minerals

Eight elements make up nearly 99 percent of Earth's crust, combining to form minerals that form rocks. Certain mineral groups are typical of certain rocks. Silica minerals predominate in most common, mostly igneous, rocks.

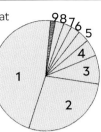
Minerals in granitic rocks

Feldspars, the most common minerals, plus quartz, micas, and amphiboles form granitic and dioritic rocks.

Group of black prismatic crystals with calcite

Single hornblende crystal

Hornblende, an amphibole, common in igneous and some metamorphic rocks

Silvery, radiating, needlelike crystals

Tremolite, common in metamorphic rocks

Amphiboles

This group of minerals is widely found in igneous and metamorphic rocks. They can be distinguished from pyroxenes (opposite) by the characteristic angles between their cleavage planes (p.48).

Colorless quartz (rock crystal)

Silica minerals

Also called silicates, these minerals include quartz, agates, and opal. Quartz is one of the most widely distributed minerals, occurring in igneous, sedimentary, and metamorphic rocks.

Feldspars

Orthoclase is found in many metamorphic and igneous rocks. Its lower temperature form is microcline.

Amazonite, a microcline feldspar

Twinned crystals of white orthoclase feldspar

Thin section of a diorite
Viewed under the special light of a petrological microscope, this diorite reveals colored amphiboles, plain gray to white quartz, and lining of gray plagioclase feldspar.

Muscovite mica

Silvery tabular crystals

Biotite mica

Micas

There are two main types of mica: dark iron- and magnesium-rich biotite mica and white or silvery-colored aluminum-rich muscovite mica. All have perfect cleavage, splitting into thin flakes.

Basic rocks

The minerals shown here are all found in basic rocks like basalts and gabbros.

Pink crystals of anorthite plagioclase feldspar

White crystals of albite plagioclase feldspar with calcite

Calcite

Albite

Green olivine crystals

Anorthite

Olivine
This silicate of iron and magnesium is typically found in silica-poor rocks, such as basalts, gabbros, and peridotites. It often forms as small grains or large, granular masses.

Crystals of olivine, from Vesuvius

Single crystal of augite

Nepheline, a feldspathoid, with calcite

Thin section of a basalt
Olivine basalt reveals brightly colored olivine, brown-yellow pyroxene, and minute gray plagioclase feldspars.

Prismatic crystal of enstatite with biotite

Greenish-black prismatic augite crystals

Plagioclase feldspars
Common in igneous rocks, these minerals (above) contain sodium and calcium.

Feldspathoids
These minerals have less silica than feldspars and typically form in volcanic lavas.

Volcanic rock

Crystal of leucite, a feldspathoid

Pyroxenes
The most common pyroxene is augite, a silicate of calcium, magnesium, and iron. Enstatite is less common.

Other groups

Carbonates and clays are two more groups of rock-forming minerals.

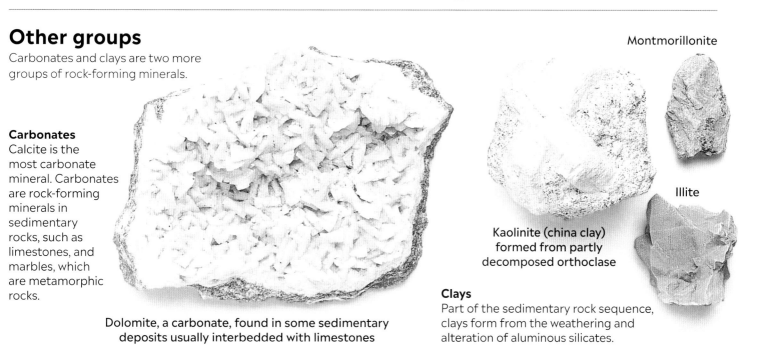

Montmorillonite

Carbonates
Calcite is the most carbonate mineral. Carbonates are rock-forming minerals in sedimentary rocks, such as limestones, and marbles, which are metamorphic rocks.

Illite

Kaolinite (china clay) formed from partly decomposed orthoclase

Clays
Part of the sedimentary rock sequence, clays form from the weathering and alteration of aluminous silicates.

Dolomite, a carbonate, found in some sedimentary deposits usually interbedded with limestones

Crystals

The word crystal comes from the Greek word *kryos*, meaning icy cold—rock crystal, a form of quartz, was once thought to be deep-frozen ice. In fact, a crystal is a solid, with a regular internal structure. Due to the arrangement of its atoms, it may form smooth external surfaces called faces. Many crystals have commercial uses, and some are cut as gemstones.

Crystals oriented in random growth directions

Light reflecting on the crystal face

Plane of intersection

Well-developed faces

"Ice" sculpted by nature

This well-formed group of rock crystals, found in Isère, France, consists of a large twin crystal and many simple crystals. The narrow ridges and furrows across some of its faces are called striations. These were formed when two different crystal faces tried to develop at the same time.

Crystal symmetry

Crystals can be grouped into seven systems according to their symmetry, which is shown in certain regular features of the crystal. For example, for every face, there may be another on the opposite side of the crystal that is parallel to it and similar in shape and size. But in most mineral specimens, it can be difficult to determine the symmetry because crystalline rocks may not always show individual crystals with well-developed faces.

What's the angle?

As the angle between corresponding faces of a particular mineral is always the same, scientists measure the angle with a contact goniometer to help identify the mineral.

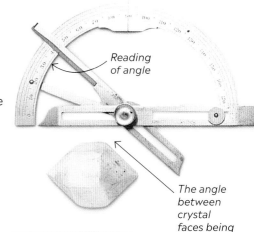

Reading of angle

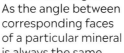

The angle between crystal faces being measured

Triclinic
This system's crystals display the least symmetry, as shown by this wedge-shaped axinite crystal.

Cubic
Metallic pyrite forms cube-shaped crystals, but other cubic mineral forms include octahedra and tetrahedra. Crystals in this system exhibit the highest symmetry.

Tetragonal
Dark-green vesuvianite crystals (also called idocrase), zircon, and wulfenite are examples of crystals in the tetragonal system.

One variety has silky luster

Rhombohedral (trigonal)
Smaller secondary crystals have grown on this siderite crystal. Quartz, tourmaline, corundum, and calcite belong to the same system.

Orthorhombic
Common crystals in this system include olivine, topaz, and barite (right), the source of barium for medical use.

Monoclinic
The most common crystal system includes gypsum (from which we make plaster of Paris), azurite, and orthoclase.

Hexagonal
Beryl, including this emerald variety, crystallizes in the hexagonal system, as do apatite, ice, and snowflakes.

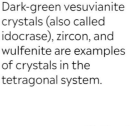

Snowflakes

Twinning

In cavities in mineral veins, crystals may grow in groups. Sometimes two (or possibly more) individual crystals appear to intersect in a symmetrical manner and are known as "twinned crystals."

Contact twins
The mineral cerussite crystallizes in the orthorhombic system, like this group of twin crystals (left).

Penetration twins
Staurolite is also an orthorhombic mineral. In this cross-shaped specimen, one twin appears to penetrate into the other.

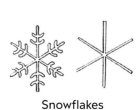

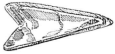

Twinned gypsum crystals get their common name, "swallow-tail," from their arrow shape.

Crystal growth

No two crystals are exactly alike because the conditions in which they develop vary. They range from microscopic to several yards long. The shape of a crystal or aggregate of crystals constitute its "habit."

Coral-like shape

White coral
Aragonite, named after the Spanish province of Aragon, can sometimes have a "coralloid" (coral-shaped) habit.

Radiating needles
Slender, elongated crystals are said to have an "acicular" (needlelike) habit. In this scolecite specimen, gray acicular crystals radiate from the center.

Fine crystal "needles"

Metallic "grapes"
Some chalcopyrite crystals grow outward from a center, and such aggregates appear as rounded nodules. The habit is "botryoidal," meaning like a bunch of grapes.

Sparkling aggregate
Hematite occurs in several habits. When it forms shiny, reflective crystals, it is said to have a "specular" habit, as in this aggregate.

Short, hexagonal terminal face at each end

Long, rectangular prism faces

Crystal columns
"Prismatic" crystals, such as this beryl crystal, are much longer in one direction than in the other two.

Soft strands
These crystals of tremolite are known to be silky and fibrous.

Equant garnet crystals

Mica schist

Thin sheets
Certain minerals, including mica, split into thin sheets and are said to be "micaceous" or "foliated" (leaflike) or "lamellar" (thin and platy).

Equal sides
Many minerals develop crystals that are essentially equal in all dimensions and are then said to be "equant." This specimen of garnet in mica schist is a fine example.

Dual form

Pyrite crystals form as cubes and as crystals called pentagonal dodecahedra, with 12 faces ("dodeca" means 12), each the shape of a pentagon ("penta" means five). Grooves called "striations" may form on the faces.

Sandy cubes

Metallic pyrite

Stepped crystals

This halite contains numerous sand grains. It grew along preferred axes, forming a stack of cubic crystals in steps.

EYEWITNESS

Salt lake, Cyprus
This shallow salt lake on the Mediterranean island of Cyprus dries up in the heat of the sun, leaving a crust of salt crystals behind. Repeated replenishment by salty water and drying out by evaporation builds up layers of salt.

Parallel lines

During crystal growth, a series of crystals of the same type may develop growing in the same direction. This calcite aggregate shows a number of tapering pale pink and gray crystals in perfect parallel orientation.

Stepped faces

Double decker

Chalcopyrite and sphalerite crystals have similar structures. Here, tarnished, brassy chalcopyrite crystals have grown in parallel on brownish-black sphalerite crystals.

Sphalerite crystals

Chalcopyrite crystals

Top of glistening pink calcite crystal group

Base of gray calcite crystal group

Hopper growth

The mineral halite (salt) is cubic, but crystals can grow from solution faster along the cube edge than in the center of the faces, resulting in the formation of "hopper crystals" that have stepped cavities in each face.

Branching metal

In a restricted space, as between two beds of rock, native copper and other minerals may grow in thin sheets. Its characteristic branchlike form is described as "dendritic."

Outline of chlorite

"Branches" of copper

Phantom growth

The dark areas within this quartz crystal formed when a thin layer of chlorite coated the crystal at an earlier stage of its growth. As the crystal continued to grow, the chlorite became a ghostlike outline.

The properties of minerals

Most minerals have a regular crystal structure and a definite chemical composition. These determine the chemical and physical properties that are characteristic for each mineral and help geologists identify it and see how it was formed.

Model showing how one atom is bonded to four others

Diamonds

Diamond
In this cubic mineral formed under high pressure, each carbon atom is strongly bonded to four others to form a rigid and compact structure. Diamond is extremely hard (Mohs scale 10).

Structure
Some chemically identical minerals exist in more than one form. For example, the element carbon forms two minerals: diamond and graphite.

Model of graphite structure

Carbon atom

Carbon atom

Graphite specimen

Graphite
In this hexagonal mineral formed under high temperatures, each carbon atom is closely linked to three others in the same layer. Built up of widely spaced layers only weakly bonded together, graphite is very soft (1–2 on the Mohs hardness scale).

Model of diamond structure

Cleavage
When crystals break, some tend to split along well-defined cleavage planes, due to their atoms' orderly arrangement.

Perfect rhomb
This yellow-colored calcite has such a well-developed rhombohedral cleavage that a break in any other direction is virtually impossible.

Thin lines show cleavage planes

Smaller crystal growing with larger crystal

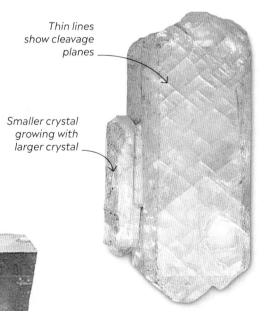

Perfect break
Barite crystals show two perfect cleavages. If this crystal were broken, it would split along these planes.

Shell-like conchoidal fracture

Fracture
Crystals that break leaving uneven, rough, or shell-shaped (conchoidal) surfaces that are not related to their atom structure are said to fracture.

Hardness

The bonds holding atoms together dictate a mineral's hardness. In 1812, mineralogist Friedrich Mohs devised a scale of hardness that is still in use today. He chose ten minerals as standards and ranked them so that any mineral on the scale would scratch only those below it.

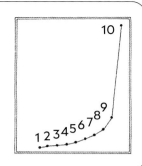

1	2	3	4	5	6	7	8	9	10
Talc	Gypsum	Calcite	Fluorite	Apatite	Orthoclase	Quartz	Topaz	Corundum	Diamond

Magnetism

Only two common minerals, magnetite and pyrrhotite (both iron compounds), are strongly magnetic. Magnetite lodestones were used as an early form of compass.

Clusters of iron filings

Natural magnet
Permanently magnetized magnetite attracts iron filings and other metallic objects, such as paper clips.

Optical

The optical effect as light passes through a mineral is due to light's interaction with atoms in the structure.

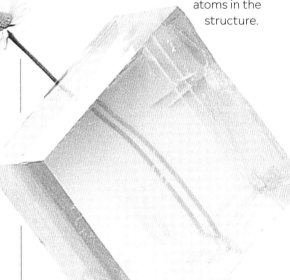

Double image
Light traveling through a calcite rhomb is split into two rays, which makes one daisy stalk seem like two.

Fluorescing autunite
Viewed under ultraviolet light, certain minerals fluoresce.

Specific gravity

Specific gravity is defined as the ratio of the weight of a substance to that of an equal volume of water. Determining the specific gravity may aid identification.

Size vs. weight
The nature of the atoms and internal atomic arrangement of a mineral determine its specific gravity. These three mineral specimens are different sizes but weigh the same, as the atoms in quartz and galena are heavier or more closely packed together than the atoms in mica.

Mica

Galena

Quartz

Gemstones

Gemstones are minerals of great beauty, rarity, and resilience. Light reflects and refracts with the minerals to produce the intense colors of gems, such as ruby and emerald, and the "fire" of diamond. Color, fire, and luster are revealed by skilled cutting and polishing for use in jewelry. Gems are usually weighed by the carat, equal to one-fifth of a gram.

Diamond

Diamond is named from the Greek word adamas ("unconquerable"). It is the hardest mineral of all and famed for its lasting fiery brilliance. The quality of a gem diamond is measured by the four Cs: its color, clarity, cut, and carat weight.

Diamond crystal

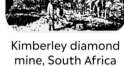

Kimberley diamond mine, South Africa

Diamonds in rock
Kimberlite is the source rock for most diamonds. It is named after Kimberley in South Africa, where it occurs in a volcanic pipe that has its roots 100–200 miles (160–320 km) deep in Earth's crust.

Kimberlite

Treasures in gravel
Until 1870, diamond crystals and fragments came from river gravels, mostly in India or Brazil. Then South Africa's diamond-rich kimberlite made it the leading supplier.

Colors of diamonds
Diamonds range from colorless through yellow and brown to pink, green, blue, and a very rare red. Table, rose, and brilliant cuts display their fire and luster to best advantage.

Crown jewel
The Koh-i-noor Indian diamond, worn here by Queen Mary, was given to Queen Victoria in 1850.

Beryl

Beautiful, hexagonal beryl crystals are found in many countries. Emerald and aquamarine, two major gem varieties, have long been exploited. Egyptian emerald mines date back to 1650 BCE.

Yellow heliodor

Aquamarine

Colorful beryls
Pure beryl is colorless. The colors are due to small amounts of impurities (trace elements). Pink morganite is colored by manganese. Yellow heliodor is named after the sun, and aquamarine is named after the color of the sea. Colors can be improved with heat treatments.

Roman beryl
The earrings and necklaces contain cut emeralds.

Pink morganite

Cut emerald

Emeralds
The best emeralds come from the emerald mines in Colombia. Perfect emeralds are very rare, and most crystals contain small imperfections (called "flaws"), such as marks, cracks, or mineral inclusions.

Corundum

Ruby and sapphire are varieties of the mineral corundum, which is colorless when pure. Tiny quantities of chromium make ruby red. Iron and titanium give the blues, yellows, and greens of sapphire.

Star sapphire
Stones with fine, needlelike crystals orientated in three directions can be cut as star rubies or star sapphires.

Sapphire crystal
Ruby tends to form in flat crystals, while sapphire tends to be barrel-shaped or pyramidal, often with zones of blue to yellow color.

The Edwardes Ruby
This exceptional crystal weighs 162 carats. It is almost certainly from the famous gem deposits of Mogok, Myanmar (Burma).

Cut ruby

Gems in jewelry
The oldest jewelry comes from burials 20,000 years ago. This late-16th-century enameled, gold pendant is decorated with rubies, emeralds, and diamonds.

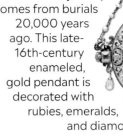

River jewels
Most sapphires and rubies come from river gravel, where gems are sorted by river currents. They are denser than rock surrounding them and so get concentrated in the gravel.

Gem sources
Australia supplies the most blue and yellow sapphires. Rubies are mined in Myanmar, Thailand, and central Africa. Sri Lanka is famous for blue and pink sapphires.

Blue sapphire

Colorless sapphire

Pink sapphire

Yellow sapphire

Clear sapphire

Mauve sapphire

Opal

Opal probably gets its name from India, from the Sanskrit word *upala* ("precious stone"). Roman jewelry used opals from the Czech Republic. In the 1500s, opal came from Central America. After 1870, Australia became the leading supplier.

Opal's rocky origins
Most opal forms over long periods of time in sedimentary rocks, like this sample from Australia, but in Mexico and the Czech Republic, it forms in gas cavities in volcanic rocks. Opal is often cut as cabochons, but the veins in sedimentary rocks are often thin. Slices may be glued onto onyx or glass to form doublets and capped with clear quartz to form a triplet.

White opal

Iridescent black opals

Color variations in opal
Opal's blue, green, yellow, and red iridescence is caused by light from minute silica spheres within the mineral. The "body" color can be clear, milky, white, or either gray or black in its most precious form.

Fire opal
The finest fire opal comes from Mexico and Turkey and is usually cut as faceted stones. It is valued as much for its intensity of color as for its iridescence.

👁 EYEWITNESS

Opal mining
An Australian miner uses a hammer to remove a thin layer of opal. Australia produces about 95 percent of the world's precious opal. It is the country's official national gemstone.

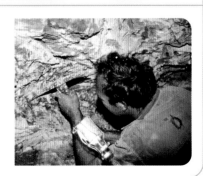

Lapis lazuli

This blue gem consists mainly of lazurite and sodalite minerals with white calcite and specks of brassy-colored pyrite.

Decorative stones

Turquoise, agate, lapis lazuli, and jade are all gems made up of many crystals. They are valued mainly for their color, evenly distributed, as in turquoise, or patterned, as in an agate cameo. Agate and jade are also tough, ideal for fine carving.

Vein of turquoise

Turquoise

Found in the earliest jewelry, turquoise gives its name to "turquoise blue," a pale greenish-blue. Its color is largely due to copper and traces of iron. The more iron that is present, the greener the stone.

Lapis crafts
Long used for beads and carvings, lapis has been known for more than 6,000 years and is named from the Persian word *Lazhward* ("blue").

Egyptian amulet
Many fine carvings have been recovered from the tombs of Egyptian pharaohs.

Purest samples
The best lapis lazuli is mined in Badakhshan, Afghanistan, where it occurs in white marble.

Turquoise ornaments
This artifact may be of Persian origin. The double-headed serpent (below) is from an Aztec necklace.

Cut turquoise
The finest sky-blue turquoise has been mined in Nishapur, Iran, for 3,000 years. Another ancient source, known to the Aztecs, is in the southwestern US, which now supplies most of the world's turquoise.

Mesopotamian mosaic
Lapis was used to decorate the wooden box known as the Standard of Ur (detail above), c. 2500 BCE.

Chalcedony

Carnelian, onyx, chrysoprase, and agate are all forms of chalcedony. Pure chalcedony is translucent gray or white and consists of thin layers of tiny quartz fibers. Impurities create the patterns in agate.

Agate
Banded agates form in cavities in volcanic rocks. Uruguay and Brazil are the main sources.

Crystals

Deep-colored band

Ancient favorite
Apple-green chrysoprase has been used in jewelry since pre-Roman times, often as cameos or intaglios.

Chrysoprase cabochon

Polished sliced agate
Microscopic crystals formed in bands as hot, silica-rich solutions filtered through cavities in porous rocks.

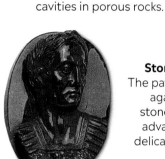

Cameo portrait
This bloodstone shows a Roman emperor.

Stone landscape
The pattern in moss agate or mocha stone is shown to advantage in this delicate cabochon.

Ornamental knife
Carnelian is a reddish-brown chalcedony and has been used in jewelry and inlay work throughout history.

Jade

Named from the Spanish *piedra de hijada* used to describe the green stone carved by the Indians in Central America, jade refers to two different rocks—jadeite and nephrite.

Rare jade
Jadeite can be white, orange, brown, lilac, or the translucent green "imperial jade."

Mughal dagger
Mughal craftsmen carved pale green and gray nephrite into dagger handles, bowls, and jewelry, often inlaid with rubies and other gems.

Chinese art
The toughness of jade was known to the Chinese more than 2,000 years ago, and this was exploited in their delicate carvings.

Tutankhamun's mask
In 1922, a British archaeologist unearthed many artifacts from the tomb of the ancient Egyptian King Tutankhamun. One of them was the pharaoh's death mask, in which blue lapis, reddish-brown carnelian, black obsidian, colorless or white quartz, and colored glass are inlaid in gold.

Nephrite boulder
Nephrite is more common than jadeite and is generally green, gray, or creamy white. Most nephrite and jadeite occur as rounded waterworn boulders, as in this example from New Zealand.

Other gems

In addition to well-known gemstones such as diamond, ruby, sapphire, emerald, and opal, many other minerals have been used for human adornment. These are just some of the stones frequently seen in jewelry, but the full range of luster, fire, and color is extensive.

Black Prince's Ruby
The large red stone in the Imperial State Crown was mistakenly called a ruby, but it is a spinel.

Small ruby

Spinel

Spinel

Red spinels resemble rubies and were once called balas rubies, after Balascia, now Badakhshan in Afghanistan. There is also a range of pink, lilac, blue, and bluish-green stones.

Blue spinel

Pink spinel

Mauve spinel

Topaz

Occurring chiefly in granites and pegmatites, some gem-quality topaz crystals are very large, weighing many kilograms. The largest stones are colorless or pale blue, but the most valuable are golden-yellow imperial topaz or pink topaz.

Yellow topaz   Blue topaz

Imperial colored topaz

Topaz ring
Pink topaz is one of the rarest and most valuable varieties of topaz. Yellow topaz is heated to turn it pink. Pink topaz was also popular in Victorian times.

Tourmaline

Tourmaline shows the greatest range in color of any gemstone, and some single crystals are multicolored. The crystal forms and electrical properties are different at each end of a crystal—this polarity is sometimes reflected in color differences, especially pink and green. Cut stones can show this variation to advantage.

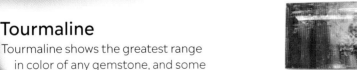

"Watermelon" tourmaline

Parti-colored tourmaline

Yellowish-green tourmaline

Mauve-gray tourmaline

Blue tourmaline

Pink tourmaline

Brown tourmaline

Green tourmaline

Garnet

Garnet is a group name for a diverse set of gems that includes almandite and pyrope (red and purplish-red), spessartite (orange-red), grossularite (orange, green, or colorless), and demantoid (green). Fine green demantoid garnet has a bright emerald color and is the rarest and most expensive of the garnets.

Grossularite garnets

Greek diadem
This section of a Hellenistic diadem dates from the 2nd century BCE and is inlaid with garnets. Its design is common to many Greek artifacts of that time.

Rose-cut stone

Garnet earrings
Rose-cut stones make attractive jewelry when set in gold, as shown by these 18th-century earrings.

 Almandite

 Essonite

 Pyrope

  Demantoid

Demantoid garnets

Byzantine relic c. 955 CE
Many Byzantine artifacts were made of gold and decorated with precious stones. Crafted in Constantinople, the Limburg Staurotheke is a container for holy remains. Featuring nine enamel panels, it depicts angels surrounding Christ on a throne, the Virgin Mary, and St. John the Baptist.

Zircon
Named from *zargoon*, the Arabic word for golden colored, zircon occurs in many colors, including reddish brown, golden yellow, yellow, green, blue, pink, and colorless. Brown zircon can be heat-treated and irradiated to colorless or blue stones popular in jewelry.

 Pink zircon

 Green zircon

 Yellow zircon

 Heat-treated and irradiated blue zircon

Peridot
This is the transparent gem variety of olivine. The proportion of iron in the mineral determines the shade of color. The more valuable golden-green and deep-green stones contain less iron than those with a brownish tinge. Peridot has been used in jewelry since classical times and originally came from St. John's Island in the Red Sea.

Amethyst
Purple amethyst is a variety of quartz. Colorless, transparent rock crystal is the purest form of quartz, and the colors of amethyst, citrine (yellow quartz), and rose quartz are caused by iron or titanium impurities.

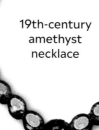
19th-century amethyst necklace

Cut amethyst

Cut peridots

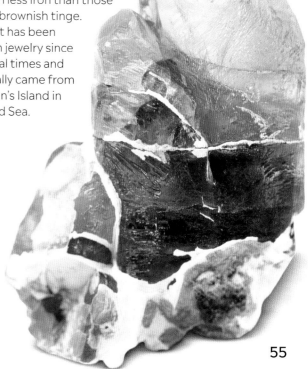

Ore minerals

Mined, quarried, or dredged from lakes and rivers, ore minerals are crushed and separated and then refined and smelted (fused and melted) to produce metal. Copper was in use well before 5000 BCE. Around 3000 BCE, tin was added to make a harder metal, bronze. Iron was even harder and was widespread by 500 BCE.

Bronze ritual food vessel from China from about 1000 BCE

Bauxite— aluminum ore

Lightweight aluminum

Aluminum is lightweight, a good conductor of electricity, not easily corroded, and used in power lines and saucepans.

Aluminum kitchen foil

Colorful copper

Brassy, yellow chalcopyrite and bluish-purple bornite are common copper ores. Because it is a good conductor, copper is used in the electricity industry, and because it is malleable (easy to shape and roll), it is good for household water pipes. It is also used in alloys with zinc (brass) and with tin (bronze).

Chalcopyrite— copper ore

Stacks of aluminum ingots

Tough iron

Hematite is the most important iron ore. Iron is tough and hard, yet easy to work. It can be cast, forged, machined, rolled, and alloyed (mixed) with other metals. Steel is made from iron.

Steel screw

Copper plumbing joint

Bornite— copper ore

Airliner partially constructed from titanium

Hematite— iron ore

Rutile— titanium ore

Strong titanium

Rutile and ilmenite are the main ores of titanium. Usually found in igneous or metamorphic rocks, these two minerals form deposits with other minerals, many of which are extracted as by-products. Lightweight yet very strong, titanium is widely used in aircraft frames and engines.

Sphalerite— zinc ore

Galvanized nail

Durable nickel

Nickel comes from deposits in large, layered gabbroic intrusions and from deposits formed by the weathering of basaltic igneous rocks. Nickeline occurs in small amounts in silver and uranium deposits where nickel is a by-product. Nickel is used in corrosion-resistant alloys, such as stainless steel, and in high-temperature, high-strength alloys suitable for aircraft and jet engines.

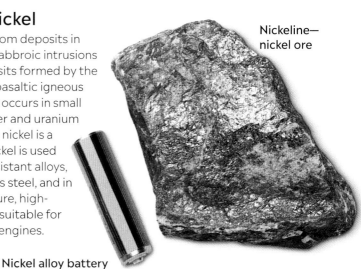

Nickeline— nickel ore

Nickel alloy battery

Black jack zinc

Sphalerite or "black jack," as it was known by miners, is the most important zinc ore and is found in deposits in volcanic and sedimentary rocks. Zinc is used in galvanizing—coating sheet steel with a thin layer of zinc to prevent it from rusting.

Cinnabar— mercury ore

Red mercury

The poisonous mercury ore cinnabar forms near recent volcanic rocks and hot springs. Mercury is very dense, has a low melting point, and is liquid at room temperature. It is widely used in drugs, pigments, insecticides, and scientific instruments.

Lead solder

Mercury thermometer

Soft and shiny lead

Galena, the main lead ore, is worked chiefly from deposits in limestones. Lead is the densest and softest common metal, with a high resistance to corrosion, but it is not very strong. It is used in storage batteries, gasoline, engineering and plumbing, and with tin in solder.

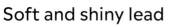

19th-century tin mine in Cornwall, UK

Crystalline cassiterite— tin ore

Workable tin

The tin ore cassiterite is hard, heavy, and resistant to abrasion. Modern uses of tin are based on its resistance to corrosion, low melting point, malleability, lack of toxicity, and high conductivity. It is used in solder and tin plate. Pewter is an alloy with roughly 75 percent tin and 25 percent lead.

Galena—lead ore

Tin can, more often made of aluminum

Precious metals

Gold and silver were among the first metals discovered. Valued for beauty and rarity, they—and platinum in the last 100 years—are used in coins to prove wealth, buy, and sell, and in jewelry and other objects.

Platinum

Popular in jewelry, platinum is also used in oil refining and in reducing pollution from car exhaust.

Sperrylite crystal
Platinum is found in several minerals, one being sperrylite. This is the largest known sperrylite crystal, found in South Africa c. 1924.

Platinum grains
Most platinum minerals occur as tiny grains in nickel deposits. These grains are from Colombia, where platinum was first reported in the 18th century.

Imperial coins
Platinum has been used as coinage in several countries, including Russia.

Platinum nugget
Large nuggets of platinum are rare. This one, from Nizhni-Tagil in the Urals, weighs 2.4 lb (1.1 kg), but the largest on record weighed 21 lb (9.7 kg).

Silver branches
Occasionally, as in this specimen from Copiapo, Chile, silver occurs in delicate, branchlike dendritic forms.

Delicate silver wires
Silver is now mostly extracted as a by-product from copper and lead-zinc mining. Until the 20th century, it was mostly mined as native metal, like the famous silver "wires" from Norway.

Silver

Long used in coinage, but less valuable than gold or platinum, silver easily loses its shine and becomes tarnished. Sterling and plated silver is made into jewelry and ornaments.

Religious bell
One of a pair, this silver Torah bell was made in Italy in the early 18th century and was used in Jewish ceremonies.

Gold

Today, this metal is used in jewelry, electronics, and dentistry, but more than half the gold mined is buried again—in bank vaults, as investments.

Crystalline chalcopyrite

South Africa
Traditional gold mines were labor-intensive.

The Great Gold Rush
Prospectors flocked to pan gold in 19th-century California; the Yukon, Canada; and Australia.

Fool's gold
Pyrite and chalcopyrite's brassy color can be mistaken for gold. But chalcopyrite, the main ore of copper, is more greenish-yellow, more brittle, and harder than gold, although not as hard as pyrite.

Chalcopyrite

Vein gold
Gold may occur in quartz veins. It is extracted by crushing the ore for a concentrate, which is then smelted.

Cubes of pyrite

Pyrite
Pyrite mostly forms cubic crystals. Crystalline rocks that don't show a crystal habit are called "massive." Pyrite is closer in color to "white gold" or electrum, an alloy (mixture) of gold and silver, than to pure gold.

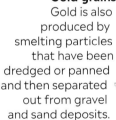

Tutankhamun's collar

Gold grains
Gold is also produced by smelting particles that have been dredged or panned and then separated out from gravel and sand deposits.

Massive pyrite

Egyptian craft
The ancient Egyptians were one of the first civilizations to master the art of goldsmithing, using solid, beaten gold. Nowadays, copper and silver are often added to gold (measured in carats) to make it harder.

👁 EYEWITNESS

Largest golden nugget
In February 1869, miners John Deason and Richard Oates found the world's largest gold nugget, Welcome Stranger, in Australia. It was 24 inches (61 cm) long and weighed 159 lb (72 kg), as much as an adult.

Replica of Welcome Stranger

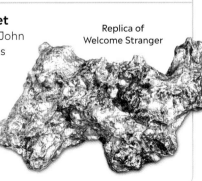

Cutting and polishing

The earliest gemstones were rubbed together to produce a smooth surface, which could then be engraved. Skilled workers, called lapidaries, cut and polish gemstones, choosing the best way to keep them as large and beautiful as possible, sometimes helped by using computers.

Grinding and polishing agates in a German workshop, c. 1800

Cutting gems

When mined, gemstones often look dull. To create a desirable, sparkling gem, the lapidary must cut and polish it to enhance its natural qualities, allowing for any flaws within.

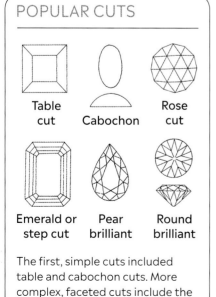

The hardest cut
Rough diamonds are marked with india ink before the first break or cut is made.

POPULAR CUTS

Table cut	Cabochon	Rose cut

Emerald or step cut	Pear brilliant	Round brilliant

The first, simple cuts included table and cabochon cuts. More complex, faceted cuts include the round brilliant cut for diamond.

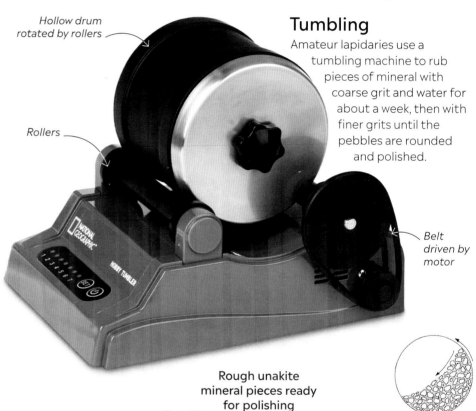

Hollow drum rotated by rollers

Rollers

Belt driven by motor

Tumbling

Amateur lapidaries use a tumbling machine to rub pieces of mineral with coarse grit and water for about a week, then with finer grits until the pebbles are rounded and polished.

Rough unakite mineral pieces ready for polishing

Grits and polishes

Grinding grits are used in sequence, from the coarsest to the finest.

Polished unakite pieces after tumbling

Tumbling action

As the drum rotates, pebbles are rubbed smooth and round.

Water added with grits

Coarse grinding grit used in first tumbling

Fine grinding grit for second tumbling

Cerium oxide, fine polishing powder, finally makes pebbles smooth and sparkling

Quartz

Because of its abundance and hardness (and hence its ability to polish up well), the silica group of minerals including quartz is the most commonly used for the production of tumbled stones.

Rough quartz ready to be broken for tumbling and polishing

Polished rock crystal (colorless quartz)

Amethyst

Amethyst makes attractive polished stones, with areas of lighter and darker purple and colorless patches.

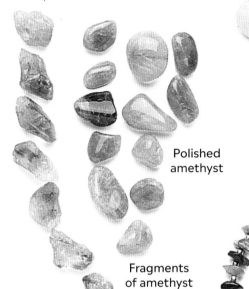

Polished amethyst

Fragments of amethyst

Polished rose quartz

Fragments of rose quartz

Rose quartz

The pink variety of quartz, rose quartz, is far rarer than milky quartz or amethyst. Most rose quartz comes from Brazil, but the US is also a key producer.

Intaglio seal

Intaglio showing detail of a horse carved into an onyx locket

Cameo showing a scene from the myth of Hercules

Necklace

Colorful tumbled stones can be made into necklaces and bracelets.

Carved alabaster stone

Carved stones

Cameos have a raised design, carved in relief, while intaglios are hollowed out.

Thomsonite

Color-banded thomsonite fragments produce unusual patterns and "eyeballs" when tumbled. The best material is found in Minnesota. Thomsonite is a reasonably widespread silicate mineral and occurs in basalt flows.

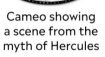
Polished thomsonite

Thomsonite rock

Assorted stones

Various mineral and rock species are suitable for tumbling. Some of the most attractive include tigereye (1), blue aventurine (2), amazonite (3), snowflake obsidian (4), Apache tears (5), moss agate (6), red-banded agate (7), sodalite (8), crazy lace agate (9), and snakeskin agate (10).

Starting a collection

Collecting mineral and rock specimens is a rewarding and popular pastime. It dates back to the amateur geologists of the 19th century, many of whom amassed impressive collections.

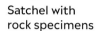

Satchel with rock specimens

Geologist's hammer (1 lb/0.5 kg)

Geologist's trimming hammer

Careful planning

Plan any field work and collecting trips in advance, using geological guidebooks, maps, and internet searches before your visit. Download useful apps (such as a compass and map) onto your phone. Make sure that you can get a signal and that your phone is charged. Get permission to visit any area or site on private land. Check tide times if you are visiting a beach to make sure that you don't get cut off by the tides. Never enter old mines or cave systems. Do tell someone where you are going and when you expect to be back.

Map

Compass

Collecting kit

Pack a geological hammer, but don't hammer unnecessarily. Take photos rather than specimens, unless you really need a few specimens for your collection.

EYEWITNESS

Young rock collectors

Anyone interested in rocks can become an amateur rock collector, or a rockhound. They can start their collections by gathering rocks based on their color, shape, or texture. Rare rocks are found sometimes, such as this agate from Brazil that resembles the popular character Cookie Monster.

Blue agate

Protective clothing

To prevent injury from flying rock and metal splinters, wear the protective gear shown here, sturdy shoes or boots, and strong, waterproof clothing.

Strong gloves

Safety helmet

Guide book

Protective goggles

Warning

When rock collecting, there are certain rules you should follow at all times: check that collecting is allowed and always obey the local rules, ask permission before entering private land, avoid disturbing wildlife, wear suitable clothing, use proper equipment, and avoid creating hazards for others.

Identification

In the field, use a x10 magnification hand lens. Indoors, a binocular microscope will reveal finer details.

Spatulas for fine work, such as cutting around fossils

Surgical knife for fine preparatory work on fossils

Palette knife for extracting small crystals from soft fossils

Cleaning

To remove surplus rock from a specimen, wash it in water and scrub lightly with a soft brush. Or sift crumbly rock like clay for small crystals and bits of rock.

Trowel for digging soft rocks

Sieve for sorting material

Paintbrushes for cleaning specimens

Recording a find

Number the specimen by placing a label with the specimen before you wrap it. Make a note of exactly where you found it, with a comment or sketch in your notebook, or take notes and a photo as a reminder. Try to include something, such as a coin or your hammer, in your photo to show the size of rocks and where you found the specimen before you remove it.

Pen

Notebook

Camera

Pencil

Transporting

Wrap each specimen individually to avoid chipping or scratching. As crystal groups are usually very fragile, pack them in tubes or boxes with wrapping and carry in collecting bags.

Sample bag

Newspaper

Bubble wrap

Plastic tube

Curating your collection

To prevent damage to specimens, store them in individual trays or boxes in shallow drawers. Keep in mind their individual needs—some minerals deteriorate in damp, heat, or light.

Boxes for storing specimens

Labels for documenting specimens

Sealable plastic bag

Did you know?

AMAZING FACTS

After astronauts returned from the moon, scientists discovered that the most common type of lunar rock is a basalt also found on Earth.

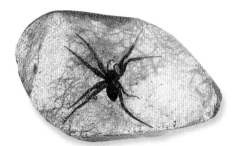

Spider fossilized in amber

Amber formed when sticky resin oozed from trees millions of years ago, sometimes trapping insects before it hardened.

The deeper into the crust a tunnel goes, the hotter it becomes. The deepest gold mines in South Africa have to be cooled down artificially so that people are able to work in them.

Devil's Tower, Wyoming

Devil's Tower, in Wyoming, is a huge rock pillar made from lava that crystallized inside the vent of a volcano. Over thousands of years, the softer volcanic rock surrounding the vent wore away, leaving the Tower.

More than 75 percent of Earth's crust is made of silicate minerals, composed mainly of silicon and oxygen.

On some coastlines made up of soft rocks, the sea carves away yards of land every year. Some villages, such as Dunwich in Suffolk, UK, have partly fallen into the sea as cliffs collapsed.

Ice can shatter rock. Granite, one of the hardest rocks, can be split by water in cracks, expanding as it freezes. The combined weight and movement of a glacier (a river of ice) can hollow out a whole mountainside.

Unaware it was poisonous, women in ancient Rome used the mineral arsenic as a cosmetic to whiten their skin.

Graphite, used in pencils, is also used in nuclear power stations. Huge graphite rods help control the speed of nuclear reactions in the reactor core.

Obsidian is a black, volcanic rock that is so shiny, it was used as a mirror in ancient times.

Rocks are constantly changed by erosion and forces deep inside Earth. Water and wind have carved out this sandstone arch over millions of years.

Obsidian

Fossil of *Archaeopteryx*

In 1861, a quarryman discovered the fossil of a birdlike creature with feathers that lived 150 million years ago. *Archaeopteryx* may link prehistoric reptiles and today's birds. Minerals don't only exist in rocks. Your bones are made of minerals too!

Prebischtor sandstone arch, Czechia

QUESTIONS AND ANSWERS

What are the most common rocks in Earth's crust?

Volcanic rocks, such as basalt, are the most common crustal rocks. Basalt forms from the more fluid type of lava as it cools and hardens. It makes up the ocean floors, which cover 68 percent of Earth's surface.

How do we know that dinosaurs existed?

Dinosaur bones and teeth have been found as fossils all over the world (as have other animals and plants). Even their footprints and dung have been preserved in rock.

Chinese nephrite dragon

What is jade, and why does it have more than one name?

In 1863, this rock was found to be two different minerals, now called jadeite and nephrite.

Why are the pebbles on a beach so many different colors?

Pebbles are made up of many types of rock, washed up from many places. Their colors show what kinds of minerals they contain.

Fossilized footprint of a dinosaur

If pumice is a rock, how come it can float on water?

Pumice is hardened lava froth from volcanoes on land and under the sea. It is full of tiny air bubbles—the air trapped inside these bubbles makes pumice light enough to float on water.

What made the stripes on the desert rocks in Utah?

The rocks are made of layers of sandstone. Over millions of years, hot days, cold nights, floods, and storms have worn away the softer layers of rock, creating stripes in the landscape.

What are the oldest rocks on Earth?

The oldest known rocks came from space as meteorites. This chondrite is 4,600 million years old, as old as Earth, and even older than the first rock to form on Earth about 4,200 million years ago.

Chondrite

Are there any new rocks forming on Earth?

New rocks form all the time, some from layers of sediment, others from volcanic activity under water and on land. Rock is constantly recycled by heat, pressure, weathering, and erosion.

What is a desert rose made from, and how did it form?

Desert rose is made of gypsum. It formed when water quickly evaporated, leaving impurities that formed crystals shaped like petals.

Desert rose

RECORD BREAKERS

- **Most valuable metal**
  Rhodium followed by palladium are the most valuable metals of the platinum group. Platinum is rarer than gold.

- **Biggest gold nugget**
  The Welcome Stranger found in Australia in 1869 weighed 159 lb (72 kg), as heavy as an adult.

- **Hardest mineral**
  Diamond is the hardest known mineral and cannot be scratched by any other.

- **Biggest stalagmite**
  A stalagmite in Son Doong Cave, Vietnam, is 230 ft (70 m) tall.

- **Biggest rock**
  Uluru (Ayer's Rock) in Australia is the biggest freestanding rock in the world. It is more than 2 miles (3.6 km) long.

Badlands, Utah

Rock or **mineral?**

Geologists classify rocks according to the way in which they were formed, in three main types: igneous, metamorphic, and sedimentary rocks.

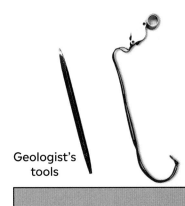

Geologist's tools

IDENTIFYING ROCKS

Igneous rocks
Igneous rocks are made from hot, molten rock from deep within Earth that has cooled and solidified. The more slowly a rock cools and solidifies, the larger the crystals can form.

Large crystals of quartz, feldspar, and mica that formed as the rock cooled slowly

Granite

Large crystals that formed as the rock cooled slowly

Gabbro

Dark, fine-grained volcanic rock that formed from lava

Basalt

Glassy volcanic rock that cooled too quickly to form crystals

Obsidian

Metamorphic rocks
New metamorphic rocks form when sedimentary, igneous, or existing metamorphic rocks are transformed by heat and/or pressure in Earth's crust. Different minerals form, depending on the amount of heat and/or pressure.

Crinkled layers

Folded schist

Fine grain size

Slate

Dark and light bands of color

Gneiss

Sedimentary rocks
Sedimentary rocks are usually made from particles weathered and eroded from other rocks. The particles, from sand grains to boulders, are deposited in layers (strata) and slowly become rocks. These rocks can contain fossils.

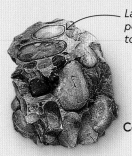

Large, coarse pebbles cemented together

Conglomerate

Iron oxide gives orange color

Sandstone

Angular fragments of rock held together by a fine, sandy material

Breccia

Formed from the skeletons of micro-organisms, chalk has a soft, powdery texture

Chalk

Each mineral is different and may have a characteristic color or crystal shape that helps us identify it. Some form crystals larger than a human, while others form as sheets or lumpy masses or grow as crusts on rocks.

Prismatic beryl crystal

Beryl
Formed deep in the crust, beryl is found mainly in granites and pegmatites. Transparent beryl is a rare and valuable gemstone—emerald and aquamarine are the best-known varieties.

Vitreous, or glassy, luster

Quartz
One of the most common minerals, quartz occurs in many rocks, often in mineral veins with metal ores. Quartz crystals usually have six sides with a top shaped like a pyramid.

Gold
Gold is a precious metal and a rare native element. Usually found as yellow specks in rocks, it often grows with quartz in mineral veins. Occasionally gold forms large crystalline nuggets.

Sapphire crystals with tourmaline

Corundum
The pure form of corundum is colorless, but it comes in many colors—rubies and sapphires are two rare forms, mostly found in river gravel. Corundum is extremely hard.

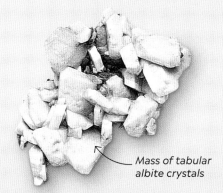

Mass of tabular albite crystals

Albite
Usually white or colorless, albite is an important variety of feldspar, a rock-forming mineral, and is often found in granites, schists, and sandstones.

Pearly luster on crystals

Cockscomb barite
Barite forms in many environments, from hot volcanic springs to mineral veins. Cockscomb barite is made up of rounded masses of soft, pearly crystals.

Orange halite crystals

Halite
Best known as rock salt, halite is one of the minerals called evaporites, which form when salty water evaporates. It is found in masses and as cubic crystals, around seas and lakes in dry climates.

Calcite
The main mineral in limestone, which usually forms in a marine environment, calcite is also found in bone and shell and makes stalactites and stalagmites.

Flat-topped, bright yellow crystal

Sulfur
A native element, sulfur crystallizes around hot springs and volcanic craters as a powdery crust of small crystals or as large crystals. Pure crystals are always yellow and soft.

Find out **more**

Rocks are all around you, on the ground, and in walls, buildings, and sculptures. The best way to find out more about them is to collect them. Going on a trip or vacation can also provide a chance to find different rocks and discover new types of landscape. Here you will find suggestions for museum collections and other good places to visit as well as a list of useful websites.

Collecting pebbles

Pebble beaches, lakeshores, and river banks are good places to look for specimens. See how many colors and types you can find. Always be careful near water.

Gathering information

Visit your local natural history or geological museum to see rocks and minerals, rare and common. Many museums also have displays on volcanoes, earthquakes, and rocks from space.

PLACES TO VISIT

THE EARTH GALLERIES AT THE NATURAL HISTORY MUSEUM, LONDON
• View amazing specimens of Earth.

THE SMITHSONIAN NATIONAL MUSEUM OF NATURAL HISTORY, WASHINGTON, D.C.
• Visit the national collections of more than 600,000 rocks, minerals and gemstones.

THE NATIONAL MUSEUM OF NATURAL HISTORY, FRANCE
• Visit the galleries used by the Sorbonne University students.

TRINITY COLLEGE GEOLOGICAL MUSEUM, DUBLIN
• Unearth fascinating geological wonders.

Earth lab

Identifying specimens

You can take rock samples to some museums for help in identifying them. The Earth Lab at the Natural History Museum in London has 2,000 specimens of rocks, minerals, and fossils, plus microscopes, qualified advisers, and an online datasite.

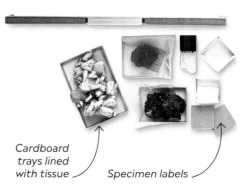

Cardboard trays lined with tissue

Specimen labels

Displaying your collection

Gently clean your rock samples with water and let them dry, then arrange them in plastic or cardboard trays or boxes. For delicate items, line the trays with tissue paper. Put a small data card in the base of each tray, with the specimen's name, where you found it, and when.

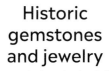

Historic gemstones and jewelry

A good place to look for jewelry and other objects carved from rock is at a museum of decorative arts, such as the Victoria and Albert Museum, in London.

Aztec jade necklace

Badlands National Park, South Dakota

History in the rocks

Sediments were laid down between about 75 and 28 million years ago, building up in layers—seen as darker and lighter bands. The oldest is at the bottom and the youngest at the top. Uncovered and carved out by more than 500,000 years of weathering and erosion, they form the landscape of the Badlands National Park.

Sculptures

People in ancient Greece and Rome used marble for their finest statues and buildings. Look at statues closely to see whether they are made from marble or another type of stone.

Marble statue of Pieta, St. Patrick's Cathedral, New York

Giant's steps

At Fingal's Cave in Scotland, visitors can see hexagonal columns of rock and a 230-ft (70-m) sea cave. In legend, the giant Finn McCool scooped a handful of rock from Northern Ireland and threw it across the sea toward Scotland, making a Giant's Causeway, from Northern Ireland to Fingal's Cave. In fact, the columns formed when basalt lava cooled and shrank, and erosion by the sea formed the cave.

Cave at Melissani, Cephalonia, Greece

Limestone caves and grottoes

Limestone caves are good places to see stalactites. There are blue grottoes on Mediterranean islands, such as Cephalonia and Malta. The Lascaux Caves in France have prehistoric cave paintings.

Glossary

ABRASION
Erosion caused by water, wind, or ice laden with sediments and scraping or rubbing against the surface of rocks.

ACICULAR
Having a needlelike form.

ALLOY
A metallic material, such as brass, bronze, or steel, that is a mixture of two types of metal.

CABOCHON
A gemstone cut in which the stone has a smooth, domed upper surface without any facets.

CARAT
The standard measure of weight for precious stones. One metric carat equals 0.07 oz (0.2 g). Also used to describe the purity of gold; pure gold is 24 carat.

CLEAVAGE
The way a crystal splits apart along certain well-defined planes according to its internal structure.

CORE
The area of iron and nickel that makes up the center of Earth. It is about 750 miles (1,200 km) in diameter.

CRUST
The thin outer layer of Earth. It varies in thickness between 4 and 43 miles (6 and 70 km).

Group of natural crystals

CRYSTAL
A naturally occurring solid with a regular internal structure and smooth external faces.

DENDRITIC
Having a branchlike form.

DEPOSIT
A buildup of sediments.

Ground worn away by erosion

ELEMENT
One of the basic substances from which all matter is made. An element cannot be broken down into a simpler substance.

EROSION
The wearing away of rocks on Earth's surface by gravity, wind, water, and ice.

EVAPORITE
Mineral or rock formed as a result of salt or spring water evaporating.

EXTRUSIVE ROCK
Formed when magma erupts as lava, which cools at the surface.

FACE
A surface of a crystal.

FACET
One side of a cut gemstone.

FIRE
In gemstones, fire is seen as a sparkle of colors caused by the dispersion of light as it enters a gemstone and splits into rainbow colors. Diamond has high fire.

FOSSIL
The remains or traces of plants or animals preserved in Earth's crust, in rock, amber, permafrost, or tar.

GALVANIZATION
A process that adds zinc to other metals or alloys to prevent them from rusting.

GEMSTONE
Naturally occurring minerals, usually in crystal form, that are valued for beauty, rarity, and hardness.

Diamond

Sapphire

GEOLOGIST
A scientist who studies rocks and minerals to find out the structure of Earth's crust and how it formed.

HABIT
The shape and general appearance of a crystal or group of crystals.

INTRUSIVE ROCKS
Igneous rocks that solidify within Earth's crust and only appear at the surface once the rocks lying on top of them have eroded away.

IRIDESCENCE
A rainbowlike play of colors on the surface of a mineral, similar to that of a film of oil on water.

KARST SCENERY
The rock formations of some limestone landscapes.

LAPIDARY
A professional gem cutter.

LAVA
Red-hot, molten rock (magma) from deep within Earth that erupts to the surface from vents of volcanoes.

LUSTER
The way in which a mineral shines. It is affected by how light is reflected from the surface of the mineral.

MAGMA
Molten rock beneath Earth's surface.

MANTLE
The layer between Earth's core and crust. It is 1,430 miles (2,300 km) thick.

MASSIVE
A term used to describe a mineral that has no definite shape.

MATRIX
A mass of small grains surrounding large grains in a sedimentary rock, or the rock surrounding a crystal.

METAMORPHOSE
To undergo a change of structure. In rocks, this is usually caused by the action of heat or pressure.

METEORITE
An object from space, such as a rock, that survives its passage through the atmosphere to reach Earth.

Meteorite

MINERAL
A naturally occurring, inorganic solid with certain definite characteristics, such as crystal structure and chemical composition.

MINERAL VEIN
A crack in rock filled by hot fluids' mineral deposits.

MOHS SCALE
A scale of hardness from 1 to 10 based on ten minerals. Minerals of a higher number are able to scratch those of a lower number.

MOLTEN
Melted, made into a liquid by great heat, especially rocks.

NATIVE ELEMENT
An element that occurs naturally in a free state and does not form part of a compound.

NODULE
A rounded lump of mineral found in sedimentary rock.

OOLITES
Small, rounded grains in limestone.

OPAQUE
Material that does not let light pass through it.

OPTICAL PROPERTIES
The various optical effects produced as light passes through minerals. This is one of the properties used to help identify minerals.

ORE
A rock or mineral deposit that is rich enough in metal or gemstone for it to be worth extracting.

OUTCROP
The area that one type of rock covers on a geological map, including the parts covered by soil or buildings.

PALEONTOLOGIST
A geologist who studies fossils.

PIGMENT
A natural coloring material often used in paints and dyes. Many pigments were first made by crushing colored rocks and mixing the powders with animal fats.

Azurite, once ground into a prized blue pigment

POROUS
Able to absorb water, air, or other fluids.

PORPHYRY
An igneous rock containing fairly large crystals set into a finer matrix.

PRECIPITATION
A chemical process during which a solid substance, such as lime, is deposited from a solution, such as lime-rich water.

PYROCLASTIC ROCK
Pyroclastic means "fire-broken" and describes all the fragments of rock, pumice, and solid lava that may be exploded out of a volcano.

RESIN
A sticky substance that comes from some plants and may harden to form amber, valued as a gem.

ROCK
An aggregate of mineral particles.

Stalactites hanging from the roof of a cave

SEDIMENT
Rock material of various sizes, ranging from boulders to silt, which is the product of weathering and erosion, as well as shell fragments and other organic material.

SMELTING
The process of melting ore to extract the metal that it contains.

SPECIFIC GRAVITY
A property defined by comparing the weight of a mineral with the weight of an equal volume of water.

STALACTITE
A hanging spike made of calcium carbonate (lime) formed as dripping water precipitates lime from the roof of a cave. Over a long period of time, stony stalactites build up in size and may hang many yards from a cave roof.

STALAGMITE
A stony spike standing on the base of a limestone cave. Stalagmites form where water has dripped from the roof of the cave or a stalactite above, slowly building up lime deposits.

STREAK
The color produced when a mineral is crushed into a fine powder. The color of a streak is used to help identify minerals. It is often a better means of identification than the color of the mineral itself, as it is less variable.

STRIATIONS
Parallel scratches, grooves, or lines on a crystal face that develop as the crystal grows.

SWALLOW HOLE
A hollow in the ground, especially in limestone, where a surface stream disappears from sight and flows underground.

TRANSLUCENT
Material that allows some light to pass through it but is not clear.

TRANSPARENT
Material that allows light to pass through it. It can be seen through.

TUMBLING
The process of rolling rough mineral pieces in a tumbling machine with water and gradated sizes of grit until the pebbles are rounded and polished.

VEIN
A deposit of minerals within a rock fracture or a joint.

VESICLE
A gas bubble or cavity in lava that is left as a hole after the lava has cooled down and solidified.

Veins of calcite

VOLCANIC BOMB
A blob of lava that is thrown out of a volcano and solidifies before hitting the ground.

VOLCANIC VENT
The central passage in a volcano, or a narrow fissure in the ground or on the sea floor, through which magma flows and erupts as lava.

WEATHERING
The breaking down of rocks on Earth's surface. This is mainly a chemical reaction, aided by the presence of water, but it may also be due to processes such as alternate freezing and thawing, or to mechanical weathering by sediment-laden wind or ice.

Index

Acknowledgments

The publisher would like to thank the following people for their help with making the book: Dr Wendy Kirk of University College London; the staff of the British Museum (Natural History); Gavin Morgan, Nick Merryman, & Christine Jones at the Museum of London for their advice & invaluable help in providing specimens; Redland Brick Company & Jacobson Hirsch for the loan of equipment; Anne-marie Bulat for her work on the initial stages of the book; David Nixon for design assistance; Tim Hammond for editorial assistance; Fred Ford & Mike Pilley of Radius Graphics, and Ray Owen & Nick Madren for artwork; Saloni Singh, Priyanka Sharma-Saddi, and Rakesh Kumar for the jacket; and Joanna Penning for proofreading and indexing.

The publisher would like to thank the following for their kind permission to reproduce their images:
(Key: a=above, b=bottom, c=centre, f=far, l=left, m=middle, r=right, t=top)

Airbus-image exm company: P. Masclet 56cb; **Ardea London Ltd.:** Francois Gohier 65tc; **Didier Barrault / Robert Harding Picture Library:** 37cr; **Bridgeman Art Library / Bonhoms, London:** 55tr; **N. A. Callow / Robert Harding Picture Library:** 13bl; **Mary Evans Picture Library:** 8tl; 12cb; 19tl; 25tl; 26crb; 28b; 32t; 34tl, cl; 36t; 37t, bl; 39cr; 40t; 41t; 50tr, cb; 57cb; 59tl, bc; **Jon Gardey / Robert Harding Picture Library:** 40b; **Ian Griffiths / Robert Harding Picture Library:** 13t; **Robert Harding Picture Library:** 13m; 18br; 22cl; 23cb; 27tr, b; 35tl, bc;

56tr; 59ca; **Brian Hawkes / Robert Harding Picture Library:** 12cl; **Glenn I. Huss:** 40cl; **Yoram Lehmann/ Robert Harding Picture Library:** 37cb; **NASA/Robert Harding Picture Library:** 6–7, 7crb; **The Natural History Museum, London:** 68cl, 68cr, 71crb; **Walter Rawlings / Robert Harding Picture Library:** 26tr. **John G. Ross/Robert Harding Picture Library:** 53; **A. C. Waltham / Robert Harding Picture Library:** 22ca; **G. M. Wilkins / Robert Harding Picture Library:** 47tr; **Alamy Stock Photo:** Agefotostock / J M Barres 24–25, John Cancalosi 9t, Chronicle 50crb, Ian Dagnall 59br, Doug Steley A 51cla, DPA Picture Alliance / Oliver Berg 37br, Jackie Ellis 17br, FLPA 18tl, Louise France 22–23, Greg C Grace 55fcl, Granger Historical Picture Archive 58r, Evgeny Haritonov 21tr, Hemis / Guy Christian 10bl, Hemis / Spani Arnaud 32crb, Heritage Image Partnership Ltd / Werner Forman Archive 31tc, Heritage Image Partnership Ltd / Werner Forman Archive / British Museum, London 52br, Heritage Image Partnership Ltd / Werner Forman Archive / Canadian Museum of Civilization 30br, Heritage Image Partnership Ltd / Werner Forman Archive / National Museum of Anthropology, Mexico City 29tc, Heritage Image Partnership Ltd / Werner Forman Archive / Provincial Museum, Victoria, British Columbia, Canada 31cla, Imagebroker / Siegfried Kuttig 15tr, The Natural History Museum 54cb, The Print Collector / Heritage Images 54tr, Science Photo Library / Francesco Zerilli / Zerillimedia 55bc, Selwyn 38–39, Charles Stirling (Travel) 29cla, Sean Xu 65bl; **Bridgeman Images:** 58clb, fclb, © Benaki Museum 55cla, © Look and Learn 32cr; **© The**